I AM

I AM

Your Guide to Mind and Body Union for Total Awareness

MAGGIE MOOR

ARCHWAY
PUBLISHING

Archway Publishing books may be ordered through booksellers or by contacting:

Archway Publishing
1663 Liberty Drive
Bloomington, IN 47403
www.archwaypublishing.com
1 (888) 242-5904

Because of the dynamic nature of the Internet, any web addresses or links contained in this book may have changed since publication and may no longer be valid. The views expressed in this work are solely those of the author and do not necessarily reflect the views of the publisher, and the publisher hereby disclaims any responsibility for them.

Any people depicted in stock imagery provided by Getty Images are models, and such images are being used for illustrative purposes only. Certain stock imagery © Getty Images.

Cover photo by Andrew Brucker.
Cover author photo by Kai York.

ISBN: 978-1-4808-7907-2 (sc)
ISBN: 978-1-4808-7908-9 (hc)
ISBN: 978-1-4808-7909-6 (e)

Library of Congress Control Number: 2019909819

Print information available on the last page.

Archway Publishing rev. date: 7/23/2019

I've learned that
whenever I decide
something with
an open heart, I
usually make the
right decision.
—Maya Angelou

Contents

Preface

I AM: Your Guide to Mind and Body Union for Total Awareness is a contemporary perspective that opens up a new understanding of the connection between your body and your brain. I present this text as a self-help guidebook for people of all ages who may be healing and rejuvenating from physical and mental anxiety, and trauma—and those who simply want to expand their overall awareness through mind-and-body union. I present this text to anyone who wants to advance their mind and lift their subtle vibration toward a state of enlightenment.

I have constructed this eleven chapter system to help clarify the process by which you can begin to incorporate this kind of awareness into your everyday perspective. Each chapter engages a psychological and spiritual discussion of specific topics that will help you learn to understand your mind and body connection and enhance a peaceful awareness in your being. For example, we will discuss topics like energetic awareness, honoring your body, acceptance, love, healthy pleasure, emotion, and so forth. At the close of each chapter, I present guided journaling exercises and meditation practices, which I have designed and found useful for helping people heal from the specific psychological and emotional issues presented in each discussion. This book will teach you to lead a happier, more joyful life with a greater sense of awareness regarding the need for a harmonious coexistence between your mind and your body. The journaling and meditation exercises at the end of each chapter will assist you in realizing a heightened sense of enlightenment in how you approach the day-to-day pressures of life.

I AM: Your Guide to Mind and Body Union for Total Awareness is different from other books on similar topics because I base my talks and techniques on Buddhist mindfulness philosophy and traditional Eastern practices, including journaling and meditation, to prescribe awareness to the body-mind connection, and a new understanding of the word sensuality. This contemporary perspective opens up an understanding of the connection between the body and the brain as a path toward total awareness, attunement to the sensuality or life force vibration in your body, and a cultivated state of enlightenment. Through these mindful practices in awareness, you will learn to clear psychic and physical blocks that stop you from being fully present and embracing the natural Life Force that moves through your organic cells, and thus lead you to experiencing heightened joys of Life.

By spending fifteen or twenty minutes per day on these practices, you will begin to experience a progression toward connecting your body with your mind. You will experience a whole new level of your inner consciousness, your natural energy, your senses, and your living pleasures. Ultimately, through following the steps and practices in this book, you will increase your awareness and capacity for self-love, by finding ways to calm your nervous system and open your sense. As you begin to incorporate these perceptions and practices into your life as an overall 'way of being,' you will find a natural experience of the sensuality, well spring of life force, that multiplies and radiates from you as an infinite, unconditional, and higher vibration manifest as pure love.

I would like to share with you how I came to write this book. We have learned in the media this year, and especially from the #MeToo movement, that almost 80 percent of our population has experienced some kind of life-altering trauma, ranging from sexual abuse and assault to anxiety, depression and addiction. This is not a personal memoir, but I want to share something about myself. If you take the 80 percent figure as truth, it is probably safe to say that you have experienced some sort of trauma in your life. Perhaps you've never dealt with it completely—or at all—but this book is meant to help you start the journey to wellness, to a sense of self you didn't have before, and assist you in building a positive outlook toward your mind and body connection. Through the system presented in this book, I hope that you can find a willingness to let go of identifying your Self as your "Story" and become inspired to develop a beautiful empowered way of experiencing your inner self, and your life.

My trauma took place when I was just a kid. As a child of ten years old, I experienced sexual abuse that in many ways dictated the direction of my life. As an early teen, I battled drug and alcohol addiction, resulting in repeated homelessness and dangerous situations. More than twelve years ago, I was in deep spiritual, emotional, and physical pain, ranging from heart palpitations to pancreatic distress. I felt so hopeless that I prayed day and night for the life force to simply be lifted from my body, and that my own heart would stop beating—and I came pretty near close. When my body was pretty limited and I had not consumed food for days, all I could do was listen to my heart beating, the slow steady ticking of time passing. Some deeper part of me began praying for some answers to this spiritual dilemma, this wish to die, and I found myself holding on with each breath.

In those moments, I slowly awakened to the realization that something bigger than my mind was keeping me alive—that beyond my wish to dematerialize, inside of me, and despite my own thoughts, was a truly deep desire, a wish to *live*. In those moments, a voice inside guided me, saying *You must find a way to honor and listen to this part of you that wants to live, You must honor the life force in your mind and body. You must honor your heartbeat.* My healing path included recovery groups and a journey to Varanasi, India, to study yoga and meditation, Gestalt talk therapy and an official degree in psychoanalysis led to work with many healers, therapists, and my own healing and rejuvenation. I focused daily on the part of me that wanted to live and thrive, listening in to *that* voice, the voice of my heart.

I slowly became immersed in filling my days with activities that brought me closer to my heart, fueled the life force within me, and brought me to understand the many techniques and practices that bring mental and physical focus and fulfillment. I have since become a national fitness athlete, recorded albums and music videos, written manuscripts, developed warm and loving relationships in my personal life, and found a passion for helping others.

My passion for helping others find a reverence for listening to their own hearts became a training and devotion to studying and developing ways of helping people heal themselves from personal trauma and connect to their internal emotional lives and natural sources of energy and power. This life experience and professional training has enabled me to work therapeutically with a wide spectrum of people who have suffered emotional and physical anxiety, addiction, trauma, and spiritual crisis. I have also learned to specialize in helping those who experience difficulties in emotional and physical intimacy and relationships, and those who seek mind and body. If making a life centered around honoring and cultivating a life centered in a union of mind and body, greater awareness, deeper inner peace and joy is what you seek, this book is your guide.

Here are some definitions that I hope help you understand the techniques I will discuss as we continue on this journey together:

- ✾ Yoga: A Hindu spiritual and ascetic discipline, a part of which, including breath control, simple meditation, and the adoption of specific bodily postures, is widely practiced for health and relaxation. Yoga offers direct, unmediated access to, or embodiment of, or participation in the divine. It is a belief in the body, and sensual experiences of the body as part of the path to the divine—not as a distraction for the divine.
- ✾ Meditation: A technique for resting your mind and finding a state of consciousness different from the normal waking state that guides you to experience levels of yourself by experiencing the center of consciousness within.
- ✾ Psychoanalysis: A method of analyzing psychic phenomena and treating emotional disorders that involves treatment session during which the patient is encouraged to talk freely

about personal experiences, especially early childhood and dreams.

✺ Gestalt therapy: Gestalt practitioners help people focus on their immediate thoughts, feelings, and behavior and better understand the way they relate to others. This increased awareness can help people find a new perspective, see the bigger picture, and start to effect changes. It often uses role-playing to aid resolution of past conflicts.

✺ Addiction recovery: A process of change through many practices of introspection, group support, and self-discovery through which an individual achieves abstinence and a continuum of improved wellness and health. It is a highly unique path for each person.

✺ Reiki: A Japanese technique, Rei means "God's wisdom" and Ki means "life force power." Based on the principle that the therapist channels energy into the patient by means of touch to activate the natural healing processes of the patient's body and restore physical and emotional well-being.

✺ Physical fitness training: Exercise that increases the heart rate to improve the body and brain's oxygen consumption, like running, swimming, weightlifting, with the correct amount of intensity, duration, and frequency that produces a significant improvement related to health and physical and mental well-being.

✺ Health and nutrition: The science of understanding the interplay of nutrients, proteins, carbohydrates, fats, and other substances in food and water in relationship to maintenance, growth, health, and disease in the body and brain. It is individual to each person and best understood for learning about your own body's needs for natural health, energy, and well-being.

✺ Primitive Mind: *Will, emotion, and reason.* Often, our Mind gets us stuck in emotion, shuts away from intellect, and remains caught in the unprocessed, visceral elements, often in anxiety. This part of our mind is limited wholly by birth and death and time (the needs and desires of the mind, life and body).

☼ Advanced Mind: *Universal consciousness, source, and energetics.*

☼ When elevated in mental awareness and deepened by intensities of experiencing communications from your body, your mind can become aware of a greater divine consciousness, something great in yourself toward which all of life tends (a harmonious and One, grounded in pure white love). Advanced Mind knows only the present: a freedom in the self-knowledge, a free delight of being. A plane of perfect knowledge that has the full integral truth of anything. It is a plane that YOU can rise to above this current limited mentality, and have perfect understanding.

☼ "Presence:" In presence you can tap into internalized powers, energy sources, that amplify the expressions of justice, peace, harmony, and love. Here you can displace the need to resort to ego fears that cause you to act in way that create difficulty, disease, ill will, resentment and negativity. In fact, as you set right the conditions of your mind and body relationship, you will attune to a higher vibration state of being, and set right the conditions of your life, which create experiences of good fortune, synchronicity, and intensely joyful feelings of lightness.

I created the system in this book with the hope that what I have learned about healing the primitive mind through awareness, and discovering a path to awakening the advanced mind, to "presence," through mind-and-body union will help you. I don't believe this book can take the place of actual in-person therapy, healing, and participation in recovery groups for those who need, but I do believe it can be used as a real and effective a guidebook for you to use as a way toward awareness, healing and awakening. I will be your guide on that journey.

Sensuality and the Advanced Mind

I hope to elucidate some of the mystery and even possible stigma placed on the word sensuality, and help you create your own, personal understanding of what your own sensuality means for you.

I have researched several definitions of the word sensuality and found that for the most part it is described as being related to the Primitive Mind. To me, sensuality does not just mean the pursuit of sex, or sexiness, or simply pleasure for pleasure's sake. To me, sensuality is a source of energy that moves through our cellular, organic bodies, resonates within our vibrational core. When we attune to this natural resonance, this vibration within, our mind and body will synchronize in Presence. Here we experience Oneness with Source, even transcendence into advanced states of consciousness.

In this book, I use the word sensuality to mean a natural, libidinal and positive energy that pulses through your mind and body all the time. The vibration of your cellular being: Your Life Force, or Chi. When you begin to understand and cultivate sensuality as a natural part of your Life Force, you may begin to honor it as a gift, and thus honor it with a reverence. Sensuality is the most natural source of energy we have. With awareness, you can cultivate sensuality within your being and it will act as a natural power that can rejuvenate, heal, calm, empower and enlighten you. There are many ways to cultivate and channel sensuality in our beings, such as meditation, exercise, expression, breath, and positive thought, all of which we will discuss in this book.

I AM: Your Guide to Mind and Body Union for Total Awareness prescribes that we learn specific perspectives and techniques and that allow us to learn to shed defenses and thus have more space within to cultivate the subtle vibration of aliveness throughout our bodies and our minds. This means creating an awareness about how to be with our own minds, and how our own minds operate. You will learn to create an awareness of the primitive mind, the many defenses, blocks, traumas, and fears that exist there. You will learn to cultivate an honor and respect for the communications your body is sending your mind, instead of defending against, splitting off from, or rejecting your body's wisdom. As we cultivate awareness of the mind and honor the experience of the body, we begin to live in a world of total awareness of a mind and body union. This creates space for the natural well spring of sensuality, and thus life force energies, in your own body to thrive and operate as a natural source of power. As you learn to experience this vibrational energy in your body that moves through all of your cells at all times during the day and night, and then learn channel this natural and rejuvenating source, and you will develop greater awareness, though a new found and total mind and body union. Here your consciousness can elevate to one of the Advanced Mind: self-love, universal love, and elevated consciousness.

Now remember, the Advanced Mind is not a state of being you will consistently exist in. You live in the material world and experience day to day pressures, so of course your mind will oscillate between Primitive and Advanced states of being. Through the perspectives and practices presented in this book, you can develop such a heightened individual awareness that you will be able to train your own mind to observe your mind and body union. As you move into observing rather than just reacting to your mind and body, you will have greater choice of perception and action. You will learn to shift your perception from fear and ego states, to higher states of pure white love and universal consciousness. Through the easy daily practices that I offer, you can find a reprieve from the egoic state of anxiety, self-will, repetitions, and fears that block your whole energetic being from attuning to Life Force vibrations within. 90% of success is staying power and consistency. You must learn to incorporate the perspectives and techniques presented in *I AM* as a way of life, and here you will find enlightenment.

Enlightenment: You are already enlightened!

I understand that many people want a "step-by-step technique to sustained enlightenment." In Hinduism and Buddhism, enlightenment is sometimes called "awakening" or the highest spiritual state that can be achieved. Enlightenment is also an education or awareness that brings change or the state of understanding something or yourself in a different way. I believe enlightenment ultimately occurs through being able to rest in the unknown. Enlightenment is in the calm acceptance of all we do not have answers for, and in having gratitude for this vast mystery of life. In this state, you are at One with the truth of the universe. It is a concept that you may understand, but have trouble putting into practice. So you see, one of my resting notes is: "Energy never dies, it is continuously transforming."

We are energetic beings who are mostly comprised of vibration that is seeking synchronicity and balance. It is always evolving, transforming, and transmuting energy. We can trust and rely on that. Change is the only constant in life, and even what is considered the ultimate and end—death—we don't know what happens. Death is another transition. The material and cellular form that contains our spiritual life force breaks down and returns to earth. We don't know what happens to spirit. Perhaps it changes in some form—perhaps it perishes. If we are enlightened or awakened to the reality of change as a constant, we must accept that change will come whether we want it to or not, for good or ill. When we resist change and fight to stay in our comfort zones, we build conflict and discontentment in our lives. I will discuss the inevitability of change in greater length in chapter 1.

One of my main goals for this book is to help you understand that we may not know how life will unfold, but we can dedicate ourselves to rooting out the physical and psychological clutter that breed spiritual and psychological discontent. I often say, "You are an eternal vastness of richness, minerals, and energy sources. You are already enlightened. All that you seek is right inside of your own mind and body." What I mean is that you can always seek to relearn and redirect your connection to your truest nature and interconnection with the universe by clearing blocks and opening your senses. These blocks and pressures will reveal themselves as we follow the principles and practices in this book. You can develop awareness by listening to your body energy, mind, heart, truth, and intuitive consciousness.

Journaling, meditation, and breath practices are a significant part of this self-awareness program. I prescribe these practical exercises to help you learn to clear psychic blocks and inspire vital growth within your cellular and spiritual form. Here, you increase your ambient energetic vibrations and awareness, opening you to contact with your inner consciousness or higher self. In simple terms, this leads to you achieving a brighter outlook on life and a greater sense of self-awareness.

I'd like to explain the importance of the exercises you will encounter as you read this book.

Journaling

The act of writing (keeping a journal) specific questions, answers, needs, feelings, desires, and so on is a time-tested and worthwhile tool for healing. Journaling creates a connection between your mind and body (mental thoughts through hands) and can open up creative pathways in your brain that otherwise would remain closed. In short, writing can heal, awaken, and enlighten us. It's an assertive act, not a passive one, like thinking we'd like to make things better—but never really doing anything about it. Journaling helps you get the clutter of thoughts and emotions out of your head and down on paper or on the computer screen. This helps you become clearer, gain understanding and acceptance of your emotions, and become more aware of what you are truly feeling, thinking, needing, and wanting. If you struggle with anxiety or emotions that revisit throughout the day and weigh you down, keeping a journal can improve your mental health. Journaling these thoughts onto paper is a helpful tool in the beginning of awareness around the perspectives that are holding you back from healing. Journaling is also helpful in that you can go back and read your passages as time progresses to gain reflective insight on your growth and the path of journey.

Now, for many, journaling can take a bit of getting used to. I have noticed that most people who are new to journaling often start with a rather linear approach, writing out the day's events like a documentation of very specific accounts of what was said in dialogue exchanges.

Of course, anything you are moved to write is beautiful and important. However, as you will find in my chapter on stream-of-consciousness journaling, I often suggest that you simply write down whatever comes into your mind and just get it out on paper. It's like weeding the garden or shining a gemstone. You get all the exterior crust out, and eventually, as you keep writing, the clarity of truth, self, and heart comes through. You become more directly in touch with yourself—in a private and intimate way. By practicing this daily, you will notice that you become more readily accessible to yourself and clearer in thought, mind, and action in your life. You are able to take the actions you need to take to achieve your truest dreams.

I understand many of us have been through intensely traumatic experiences that will affect how we feel about our own bodies. Let's try to listen to the internal voices and beliefs we have created due to these traumas.

Meditation

Meditation is the simple act of quieting and focusing your mind so that negative thoughts can pass. You can attune to the inner consciousness or life force vibration in your body. Here, a stillness occurs. MRI scans show that meditation causes the mind to secrete endorphins that have positive effects on the body. This helps the brain's stress levels, and fight-or-flight responses appear to shrink. There is an overall sense of well-being, positive emotion, serenity, and calmness in the body-and-mind connection.

There are many different techniques to meditation. Some find it best when walking, running, swimming, or practicing yoga. Some prefer to focus on a mantra or a spot in the forehead that gives the mind a resting place. Mind and body union meditations are designed to help you attune to the natural rhythm and flow of your pulse and life force energy, experience the sensations in your body, and listen to your heart. Meditation is one of the best ways to get in touch with your truth. Meditation can help you attune yourself to elements of yourself that have been hidden. Though it may seem counterintuitive because it often feels that the self is suppressed during periods of profound meditation, a clear mind is an absolutely necessary part of deep introspection. The more attuned you are to the universal energy flowing around and within you, the better equipped you are to determine the roles you are meant to play during your lifetime. Meditation can help you achieve your goals by giving you a platform from which you can examine the impact your choices have had on the world around you and the way in which those consequences have manifested in your own experiences. When you feel yourself turning inward, your dedication to the principle of meditation will help you make the most of your introspective efforts.

Meditation can also give you a platform from which you can examine the impact your choices have had on the world around you and the way in which those consequences have manifested in your own experience. When you feel yourself turning inward, your dedication to the principle of meditation will help you make the most of your introspective efforts.

Choosing to engage in this meditative state with the clear intention of seeing where your attention is led, finding your truth, and valuing what the messages are that you hear and the intuitions that come through is nourishing for your soul and your spiritual alignment. Choosing to engage in this kind of restorative activity on a regular basis prioritizes your own care and spiritual health. It will keep you feeling strong and vital.

Taking proper care of your body and self will create a happy, optimistic mind-set and make you feel more inspired to make a positive contribution to the world; that will help your soul feel more nourished. If you devote some time and attention to your own self-care today and every day. That will enable you to serve others with joy, which will bring you joy—and bring the universe more joy—and allow your soul to vibrate on a higher level.

Breath

When you breathe deeply, it sends a message to your brain to calm and relax. Here, your nervous system balances, allowing your body to fully exchange incoming oxygen with outgoing carbon monoxide. Shallow breathing can make you tired and cause your outlook to become negative. Deep abdominal breathing opens your diaphragm, and deep breathing helps you relax, detox in your cells and organs, increase cardiovascular capacity, which helps with weight loss and burning fat, eases pain in tight muscles, and brings mental clarity.

Breathing with the mental intention of experiencing your body sensations creates a connection between your mind and your body and a path to total awareness through maintaining harmony with the unknown, the ever-changing unfolding of the present moment. We are able to reconnect with the internal flow of vibration we felt so easily as children because breathing deeply balances the nervous system, and we move beyond anxiety-induced limitations and fears and into feeling the life force. I will talk more about the benefits of deep breathing for healing anxiety and trauma as we move through guided meditations.

Freedom

Now, I will discuss many philosophical, metaphysical, scientific, physiological, and spiritual points in this book. Most importantly, and I will say this several times throughout, is that you are focused on becoming present to yourself. Listen to yourself with the sensitivity that you would if a child were asking for food or water. Truly listen with an open mind, hungry to expand on your vast and unlimited potential for awareness. If you consistently allow your mind to fall back on preconceived notions, negative thoughts, victimhood, or judgments, you will find yourself stuck. Don't be afraid to allow new thoughts, perspectives, and feelings to emerge. Keep in mind that this often happens to a person who is afraid to explore their own rich, inner life. Often, the false self—a façade created by the psyche to make an appearance in society so that we fit in, yet lacks the ability for spontaneity or change—fears the unknown and tries to mask our true self. This sense of self is based on spontaneous, authentic experience and a feeling of being alive, having a real self. The false self may not want to see or express aspects of ourselves that we may be ashamed of, afraid of, or self-conscious about that others may see through us to our innermost core. Hence, the mind will create defenses that will block life force and intuitive flow in your mind and body. This will result in blocks that hold you back from transforming the energetic vibration we need to heal or are called to transform. I will explore more of these concepts as we move forward.

Are you comfortable with the inevitability of change within me? Are you repressing your own vast potential for growth and enlightenment? This can be a conscious choice. If you are aware of how you react to your own personal, private, and inevitable change, you will gain greater clarity and choice. You will be given the opportunity to clear out fixtures created by your false self and find a clear and fluid true self that will you allow you to be the vast-potential, limitless being you truly are within. This self-awareness I am guiding you through is grounded in the acceptance of inevitable change in and of itself. Allow yourself to explore your vast and rich inner world with all the freedom of the universe.

A New Way of Life

I AM offers an evolutionary journey toward enlightenment for anyone who is seeking total awareness or healing from mental and physical anxiety, addictions, or emotional and physical trauma. I hope that embarking upon this journey together culminates in the fulfillment of your purpose of being: to heal and energize yourself and other human beings and find your authentic place within the world.

As human beings, no matter what we have been through or are suffering from currently, we have the inner wellsprings of vitality and love to cultivate our own ability to follow the natural flow of truth in our bodies, minds, and spirits and find mind-and-body awareness. With this book, by mastering the healing power and wisdom of ancient and modern spiritual perspectives and the specific mind-and-body practices I will impart to you, you can forge a new beginning in your experience of work, play, love, and service.

I welcome you to join me as your trusted guide as we embark upon this healing journey toward mind-and-body union for total awareness and enlightenment. This is a new way of life. Life is quite beautiful, and I am so blessed to share this with you. With blessings, lightness, wellness, and love.

Chapter 1

Energetic Awareness

In this chapter, we will look at metaphysical and philosophical concepts that will help you understand concepts presented in the rest of this book. Topics like enlightenment, synchronicity, space-time continuum, chaos theory, and somatic awareness will be explored. Understanding and contemplating these concepts will aid you in your journey toward healing and awareness through mind-and-body union. At the close of this chapter, I will offer a simple guided meditation to help you become better acquainted with the benefits and practical technique of deep breath.

Enlightenment Matters

I want to make one careful point here. Ultimately, we seek to understand and cleanse ourselves of psychic blocks because we know that if we remain blocked psychically by things like troubling resentments, enmeshed familial relations, and past trauma, we remain stuck in repetitive psychic thoughts, shames. This creates a mind-and-body separation due to a wish to leave the self rather than commune with the self. When we commune with our essential selves, we develop a receptivity that allows us to listen and love ourselves and others more deeply. This creates deeper pools of mind-and-body energy and inspiration to continue manifesting abundance in love, work, and play in our lives.

> Be loving toward your body, befriend your body, revere your body, respect your body, take care of your body, it's nature's gift.
> —Osho

As a dedicated follower of spiritual practice, you will learn to see these blocks as educational tools and want to understand them as gifts for deeper energetic transformation, allowing time, patience, and awareness. Energy never dies; it only transforms, and we don't transform fluidly when we allow ourselves to live imprisoned by psychic blocks. The feelings that arise can be painful, but support, patience, dedication to deep cleansing, and balancing can bring great freedoms and awareness that we never knew existed or were possible.

Let us train our bodies to gently contain more and more spirit, gradually allowing ourselves to become more alive, to be here with what is. This enlightenment is the true path to spontaneous presence.

Mind-and-body energy is channeled through breath, movement, intention, motivation, and action. Energy creates a passage for the stimulation within your body to reach your brain and mind. Progressive transcendence requires cleansing ourselves of psychic blocks so that we have renewed, healthy, vital cells; an emotional ability to love and listen; and inspiration to continue working toward goals.

Energy and Synchronicity.

I understand that the word energy is used a lot, especially in the realm called new age. Let's discuss the word. Energy is the most basic phenomenon in our universe. We are surrounded by energy; our bodies are full of energy. Energy is our life force. Energy is vibration, woven throughout the body, mind, earth, and universe. This is the basic philosophy of spiritual practice and healing techniques. Energy is the unifying force interconnecting all of us with a higher vibrational consciousness.

Everything in the universe is made up of energy vibrating at different frequencies. Each of these levels has a vibrational frequency that creates your overall vibration of being. Yes, energetic vibration is the unifying force interconnecting us all. Ultimately, all vibration wants to achieve synchronicity.

Energetic vibrations attract similar vibrations. The human body and outer experience are comprised of 99 percent energy and 1 percent matter. The energetic vibration has the greatest weight and pull on your life's outcomes because all vibration wants to achieve harmony or balance. When you are focused on cultivating a higher vibrational consciousness, you may find yourself experiencing a lot of meaningful coincidences that seem to have no obvious causal relationship. Carl Jung called this "synchronicity."

Some people believe that these signs will show you how aligned you are with intuition and emotion. Carlos Castaneda called it "the path with heart." Synchronicity is what all vibration ultimately wants to achieve. Energetic vibration wishes to move into union, love, empathy, and survival of the species. However, if you are hanging on to blocks and defenses, you will be aligned with like vibrations. Your energetic body will move into harmony with like-minded people and events. If subtle energy bodies are cultivated through melting blocks and raising your vibration, your body and mind move toward balance, unity, and higher states of wisdom that promote your survival. You have unlimited power and energy, but this energy will not be revealed until you raise your vibration to the level of consciousness in which this energy exists.

Energetic Awareness in Society

In the West, hospitals and rehab and healing centers use therapeutic touch to generate cellular growth in diseased or maimed bodies. Reiki is an energy healing technique that has become more widely accepted. Emotional release practices such as talk therapy and physical movement have been shown to have healing effects on diseased tissue. We are becoming more attuned to practices like yoga. We also have more interest in:

☼ Acupuncture: An ancient Chinese healing practice of placing thin needles beneath the skin on specific parts of body's meridian lines (channels of energy flow or life force, called Chi), to relieve pain and stress.

- ❁ Acupressure: A Chinese therapy where the practitioner applies of pressure along certain points on the meridian. It is thought to clear energetic blocks and restore balance.
- ❁ Tai Chi: A Chinese tradition, often described as meditation in motion, promotes Chi flow through gentle, constant motions.
- ❁ Qigong: Ancient Chinese health method that combines movement, meditation, and breathing to increase the flow of Chi (vital energy) in the body. It is meant to treat bone problems, cancers, and stress.
- ❁ Feng Shui: Chinese science and art of decorating your home or workplace based on energetic principles to create a space that enables people to be most productive and generate the most abundance.

Yes, at the core, you are a cellular structure pulsing with energetic vibration and chemistry. This whole planet and what we know of our galaxy are comprised of atoms and molecules that repel and bond with each other. Everything, including the galactic energy that holds all of the planets in synchronized rotation and all other forms of light and life around you are comprised of that same wobble.

Chaos Theory

We know there is a randomness to life that makes our existence seem chaotic, out of control, and beyond our ability to predict. And that's right. Chaos does exist in a balanced universe, just as matter and antimatter exist. If we accept that chaos coexists with harmony, we will be better able to handle the unexpected.

Dichotomy

Chaos and synchronicity are the fundamental forces that create growth. Look at our sun. It is a sphere of hot plasma with basically an electric generator inside. The sun is internally expounding itself in convective motion and blowing itself up with tiny atomic bombs.

The expansion of pressure creates electric currents and a magnetic field that makes the sun the most important source of energy for life on earth. The balance between chaos and synthesis gives the sun power to shed just the right amount of light and heat upon this planet so that we can all survive.

Humans are the same. We all experience a constant wish to merge, bond, and expand—and then separate, individuate, and retreat. Vibration constantly seeks synchronicity through breakdown. This happens inside our bodies all the time. The combination of chaos and synchronicity allows us to transform, find new areas of perspective and action, and adapt and survive. Tuning in to this visceral experience and emotional understanding of ourselves is the basis for mind-body synergy. This is what is happening.

Is this all there is? Is there more?

Many anxieties are related to philosophical questions about life, death, where we came from, where we are going, and why. These are questions that the unconscious mind may be constantly negotiating as we move through daily life. This is because our unconscious has a primitive urge to expand and bond beyond the limitations of our own physical bodies. Isn't the meaning of life one of the most profound and elusive mysteries of all, unknown to even the greatest of historical thinkers? Of course, no one has the answers to all of this, and anyone who tells you they do is most likely mistaken.

If you want a finite and linear answer to why you are here, why any of us are here, and how, you are welcome to look and feel backward or forward. The answers you will get—or not get—will be very different at different times of your day and life, and they will always serve to satisfy different existential needs. I am aligned with this soothing understanding that we are here to transform energy. That is all.

We are here to be and learn to be as present in our mind-and-body union and life force energy as possible so that we can be as clear as we can in this transformation of energetic vibration. This does not really answer the question in any kind of linear fashion. I simply suggest we become profoundly and romantically involved with the concept that we don't know and that the mysterious force of nature that has given us life is to be revered and given service to in the form of love.

Learning to honor the unknown rather than conquer its reality, and learning to be of service to the love in your hearts, minds, and bodies, so as to help fortify the interconnectedness we all share in the life-force continuum rather than diminish ourselves and others, is the best motivation toward living and being for whatever time we are here that I can prescribe. Shall we agree to dedicate ourselves to this healing and awakening process as we move on together in this book?

Space-Time Continuum

A Native American friend said, "Past, present, and future are all happening at once, inside us."

In a letter to a deceased friend's family, Einstein said, "The distinction between past, present, and future is only a stubbornly persistent illusion." Einstein's theory of special relativity (1916), normally applied to the speed of light, proposed new concepts for space and time interweaving into a single continuum known as space-time:

> Everything moves at a same rate, in relation to one another. The speed of light in a vacuum is independent of the motion of all observers. Events that occur at the same time could occur at a different time for another. In certain higher gravitational fields, sometimes time dilates to such intensity that rays of light actually bend.

This is precisely the theory that would describe the experience of transcendence. Transcendence means to go beyond, which is often described as a spiritual state of going beyond physical needs or limitations. In psychology, self-transcendence means going beyond a prior form or state of oneself. In the mystical realm, a transcendent experience is thought of as a particularly advanced state of self-transcendence, in which the sense of a separate self is abandoned, and often is described as a feeling of union.

In terms of a space-time continuum, "past-present-future-beyond" is happening inside you at all times, cultivating the ability to tune in to the vibrational pulse happening in your body all the time, and thus allowing the nervous system to calm and balance, would allow your mind and body to open to this part of your unconscious mind, soul, or spirit that is always simultaneously experiencing past, present, and future, and beyond.

The Future

Now, let me clarify. Some would argue that we can't really experience our future. Some would argue the future is experienced by the mind and body through a projection. This is true, and it is not true. Firstly, I will explain what I mean by projection because it has two meanings:

- ✷ A projection is a scientific or linear evaluation of the future based on current events.
- ✷ Psychological projection is the mind painting a picture of reality or future events, which could be true or not true, in which the ego defends against accepting certain impulses or characteristics in themselves and attributes these traits to others, thereby coloring their idea of what will happen in the future.

In either definition, it is considered a projection of the mind when we envision our future.

In fact, fMRI scans show that the unconscious mind or brain makes decisions almost seven seconds before the actual body goes into motion. As energetic beings, we are vibrationally tuned in to what is going on around us, what is moving toward us, and what essentially is in the future on a much higher level of awareness than our conscious brains can compute.

Even if brain scans can predict our decisions seven seconds ahead of time, it is still us making the decision. Our cells are aware of this energetic vibration. Many philosophers and spiritualists believe a decision is made in that part of ourselves, the soul, that is not bound by time. The decision is made and has to pass through several layers, filters, or delays before registering in what we call consciousness. Maybe we—as energetic beings—can go forward and backward in time since it is relative to the situation.

Then there is the concept of a premonition. A premonition occurs when a person thinks in the mind that a future event will suddenly play out and then it comes true. Premonitions often feel like a simple recollection of something or someone—or having a thought or idea—and often go unnoticed. A premonition can be attributed to both kinds of projections I stated above and can border on suspicion if we are not clear and careful in our thought processes. A projection can also be attributed to the soul's energetic attunement to the vibrations moving toward our being in this time-space continuum.

Healing and Rejuvenating

In our process of healing anxiety and trauma, we begin to see that these emotional conflicts can color our ability to experience transcendence because we are carrying a negative energetic charge and projecting the expectation of future trauma. This is not our fault. We simply need to be compassionate toward that wounded inner child and heal.

We can heal the past by coming to terms with it, and we can heal by focusing on quieting the mind, feeling body sensations, and settling into the organic flow of life force within. This rejuvenates our well-spring of vitality and reminds us that we are constantly changing, and able to transcend our reactions to the past by allowing the separation of mind and body to unify. Transcending the ordinary conscious concept of self through connecting to the mind-body continuum allows for accessing higher consciousness and intuitive knowledge. This intuitive knowledge leads us to understand how our souls best synchronize right now, in the present, in this, our, lifetime. The present is really all we are, and it is a gift.

Attuning Your Organic Vibration

Remember yourself as a child. As newborn children, most human beings knew an innate confidence in some capacity. You understood viscerally that primary care was present, and some desire or internal stimulation told us when to feed, walk, or talk. This body stimulus is experienced as pulsing vibrations or movements within that drive us into action when we experience needing or wanting. Desire is a drive that propels us toward survival.

As children, most of us—even those with extremely traumatic early childhoods—have felt free at one time or another, connected to ourselves, and able to feel a part of the flow of energy in our bodies without questioning it or feeling in peril with a fight-or-flight impulse. For very little children, this internal joy usually manifests in creativity, play, and connection to primary caregivers, even in nontraditional settings. Through touch and the provisions derived from primary care, children feel a deep connection to this internal desire for life. As we grow into adulthood, we often lose this easy relationship with our source and desire due to fear for survival. We begin to try to think our ways out of the fear instead of feeling.

Somatic Awareness

Somatic awareness is learning to feel your body. Somatic awareness is very important for healing anxieties and traumas in your mind and body, and developing an attunement to the natural sensuality flowing through you at all times. By developing a somatic awareness throughout your day, even in stressful situations, you can learn to stay present instead of regressing into an old wounded state. In this place of awareness, you can feel and release negative self-talk, which we will go into further discussion on later. In a state of somatic presence, you can begin to allow pleasurable feelings to nourish and heal you. You can learn to trust your body to tell you what you need in any given moment. In a state of somatic awareness, you will be able to experience deeper intimacies with friends and lovers because you will be more sensitive to feeling the experiences they are having in their bodies. Together, through a vital synchronicity of energies, you can move toward organic healing and rejuvenation.

A large part of what I am going to teach you in the practical guided breath and meditation and breath exercises in this book has to do with somatic awareness. I want you to (re)learn to and redirect your connection to your truest nature by opening up your awareness through experiencing your senses. Through mindful breath and somatic body awareness, you can learn to move out of the cerebral, linear mind and into attunement with your body. This is what I call true presence of mind, body, soul. Let's keep reading—and you will learn how!

Let's start with a simple mindful meditation breath practice. Get comfy with this practice. You will return to this practice each time you begin a meditation. Soon, it will become a part of your new way of being throughout each day.

Mindful Meditation

Practice 1

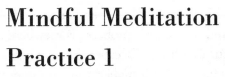
Breath

Begin a breathing practice. Think of this awareness like a muscle you are building. Here is a ten-minute mindfulness breath meditation. Practice it three times a week.

The function of breathing is to bring fresh air into the lungs and exchange it for stale or used air we no longer need, keeping the body in a constant state of renewal. Drawing in the new and releasing the old cleanses subtle or energetic body. Do not become energetically stagnant. When we limit the cleansing and renewing properties of breath, we become unwell.

As you read, start to notice your breath. Very simply, as you inhale, notice where your body expands. What part of your body are you breathing into? Release as you exhale, feeling the warmth of your breath traveling through you. There is no right or wrong; it is just about noticing you and where you are now. When you breathe in, do you like to breathe in through your nose or mouth? It can change at different points during the day. Accept the present moment now. Notice whatever is happening in your body now. We can expand and deepen from this place.

If you don't breathe deeply yet, ask, "Why? Am I holding my breath out of fear? Do I fear feeling my own body/energy/emotion?"

If you take a nice breath through your mouth, you might be able to breathe a little bit more deeply. Open your mouth and breathe. Inhale and notice. It is probably somewhere right in the center in your diaphragm because that is where breath normally goes. It may be a little bit higher, in your upper chest, or a little bit lower if you are naturally attuned to yogic breathing, swim, play a wind instrument, or just have a nice, deep breath naturally.

You can decide where in your body you send breath. As you inhale, imagine that your breath is going right into your center diaphragm and expanding like a balloon. Sometimes when we inhale, we actually suck in our center for some reason. That is how some people breathe. The really natural, correct state of physical balance is through expanding. Just imagine that your diaphragm is like a balloon that is expanding as you inhale. As you exhale, feel the heat of your breath moving up toward and through your heart, and out your throat and mouth. It is acting like an internal massage.

Notice if your heart is beating rapidly. Your heartbeat will start to slow if you count when you inhale. One, two, three—and exhale. One, two, three—through your mouth. You don't need to hold your breath after you inhale or exhale. Let your breath be one continuous, fluid movement of expansion and release and expansion and release.

When you inhale, count in your mind: one, two, three, exhale. One, two, three, find your own rhythm. Be aware that your body, mind, and breath are all connected. Feel your feet on the ground and notice that your body and mind want to move into a state of presence together. It is a natural flow. Feel your breath opening and the heat of your breath washing through your body as you exhale. Notice that you can now breathe even more deeply, maybe even down into your lower diaphragm and upper abdomen.

Imagine that your breath is moving more deeply into your lower abdomen when you inhale, into your pelvis, your lower back, and very base of your spine. You will probably feel more heat in your body the more deeply you inhale. Your inhalation will naturally expand deeply in your pelvis, especially when you imagine that your breath is opening there. Place your hand across your lower pelvis, like a triangle between your pelvic bones. Breathe.

Putting your awareness on these simple moments will help quiet the noise between your ears. If you find yourself actively trying to process, judge, and label, allow your senses to open. Touch, taste, smell, and feel the sensual movement of your breath inside your body. In this quiet inner space is inspiration for vital life energy. This is what it means to become truly present.

Try to play with that this week. Allow this awareness to become natural to your everyday experiences. Throughout each day, find moments. Slow down and notice your breath. This practice alone will organically begin to shift your awareness to a healthier mind-set and choices, fewer cravings for negative self-talk and heavy foods and more cravings for self-love, nature, and exercise.

Chapter 2

Honoring Your Body

In this chapter, we will look at a number of specific terms and practices that are essential to having a positive relationship with your body. I will explain how positive and negative self-talk affect your mind and body, why honoring your senses helps you love your body, and how physical fitness can become your friend. The concepts in this chapter are core elements for the foundational healing of trauma, awakening the body-and-mind connection, and developing an understanding of the benefits of total presence and awareness in daily life. At the close of this chapter, journaling and meditation practices will lead you through practical questions and techniques to help you become attuned to your senses for total mind-and-body union.

Life Force and Your Body

I often reference life force because I want you to develop a relationship with experiencing your own life force—within your cells, veins, heart, organs, being, and body. Life force, or as the Chinese healing arts call Chi, is an undeniable energy that mysteriously makes your heart beat and your blood flow. It is in all organic matter, throughout the universe, and it connects us all, beyond race, color, gender, and form.

> One who realizes the truth of the body can come to know the truth of the universe.
> —Osho

Life force is also an intention that circulates through you into action. Cultivating an ability to resonate with the visceral aliveness in your cells, brain, gut, and heart will guide you into a feeling of a greater source of life, beyond your own mind and will, and transport you to an experience of interconnectedness between your mind and body and all living beings. This helps you move out of an anxious mental state and into a gift. The gift is presence. When you are in tune with your body, you are present, which brings confidence in the organic, synchronistic flow of life force.

How do we free ourselves from unnecessary fear and other unhealthy patterns? Why, even after years of thinking and talking about the past, doesn't time heal all wounds? Because most of us in this culture are stuck in our heads. Healing, whether physical or emotional, happens in our bodies and not our minds. If we allow ourselves to simply feel our feelings—as bodily sensations—our bodies take it from there. It knows how to heal.

Somatic awareness is a cultivated ability to tune your body. Learning to tune in to your body is the pathway for grounding in the present. Many religions are focused on spiritual essence being above you and not in your body. I will never teach you this. Like all animals, we are self-regulating organisms. We are biologically designed to recover from the stresses and wounds of life. We're designed for some pretty traumatic things.

If you only step back and let your body do what it's knows best, it will take care of you. You are designed to recover. Denying your body stops the vital growth of life. If we cut off from our bodies, we are essentially cutting off from our very own life force. Let's try to unlearn any nonsense you may have been taught about you and your body. Let's focus on your relationship to your body as a pathway to experiencing your energetic being and a pathway to total awareness: transcendence.

Positive and Negative Self-Talk

Let's become friends with our bodies. Trust your body. Your self is right there, ready to help you, for free. It's always been there, but it's also easily drowned out by internalized, negative self-talk.

Self-talk is the way that your mind communicates with your body. If you talk to your body negatively, you will be cut off from your body. Most of us were socialized in a culture that for many years has separated flesh and sprit and chastised the body as the abode of evil instinct. At the same time, we are seduced by the media's sex symbols that urge us to appear attractive and act sexy. Some people spend an lifetimes repressing their bodies—living in a shame-based or repressed state—regarding their emotions and bodies.

All too often, we are stuck with a layer of self-criticism that subtly harms our ability to understand and cherish our own bodies and emotions. We listen to a thousand voices, inside and out, telling us what's wrong with us. If you are antagonistic or hateful toward your body and mind, you will send damaging messages to your soma, or cellular structure, and this creates pockets of imbalanced vibrational pulse. This is the beginning of becoming miserable, closed down, and ill. Negative self-talk increases the likelihood of sustained injury and disease. For example, if we say to ourselves that we're fat, we immediately feel badly. And it's our own doing via self-neglect and abuse. We can own the fact that losing weight is a good idea for the health of our bodies and hearts, but we'll never be able to circulate our life force into positive intention if we dwell in the negative realm.

When we allow our minds to mistreat our bodies, our health, love lives, and love of life diminish. Fortunately, as soon as we trade in this self-talk for some genuine listening, our bodies jump to attention and move toward a healing state of rejuvenation. Decades-old issues immediately begin to dissolve, sometimes overnight. Pain simply dissipates and is no longer held in place by self-defeating judgment. You look and are years younger. You are experiencing life with the joy and peace you knew before the hurt. You are back to being the natural, loving animal you were born to be.

Love Your Body

The body is your beginning. Yoga masters say that the body is the location of an unfolding drama. Matter ascends toward spirit, and spirit incarnates in matter. The body is your temple, the abode of a unique divinity—yourself. As the one in charge of the temple, you honor it by keeping the temple clean and healthy so that it can nurture and express the divinity within.

The good news is that it is never too late. Your natural energy and vitality are yours to cultivate at any age. You can rejuvenate yourself at any point in your life, and your cells will begin to grow toward a healthy, balanced vibration. They want to! First, we must learn to reenter our bodies by becoming conscious of the interplay between the mind and body. Negative emotional patterns, intentions, and actions work against your internal truth, and block your natural energy and vitality. How do we shed these blocks and cultivate life?

Honor Your Senses

Your essence is empowered by what your heart identifies with most deeply. This wellspring of inspiration is what I refer to as "ever-changing flow of love and the dance of life's light." The grace with which we carry ourselves conveys a confidence that emanates from a sense of vital well-being and natural self-appreciation. Your body is your intimate friend—accepted and cared for and cherished— regardless of age, shape, or color.

Physical Fitness

While you do not need to have bulging muscles or shapely curves, it is important to achieve optimum physical well-being through a healthy diet, physical exercise, deep breathing, and relaxation. Being weak and out of shape will leave you feeling tense, anxious, and distracted. Tension leads to chronic restriction of circulation of blood and energy in the body. You will not have sufficient energy, concentration, or stamina to prolong and consciously guide your living experience.

Put some energy into learning what your body needs to run at its finest performance. Daily exercise, lots of clean water, clean food, and positive thoughts are good to develop.

We acknowledge such pleasures as eating good food or enjoying a long walk in the countryside, and we actively encourage such pursuits. However, we are often not taught much about the pleasures we are able to receive with our bodies. Sadly, these blocks create obstacles to full enjoyment of sensual energy and the ability to enjoy therapeutic pleasure.

I beckon you to value the creation and maintenance of a fluid, supple body! I want you to learn to value cultivating and maintaining a body that is capable of changing positions easily and moving through the world (as much as possible!) without psychic or physical discomfort.

Energy only transforms. It never dies, which means you can always shift and change. You are never locked into one belief system or physical mode of being. There is always room to grow and change—even within limitations. Look at our amazing Invictus Games athletes, who have overcome trauma from war wounds and become amazing Olympic athletes. The power of the mind and body in union is limitless.

Awareness Is the Beginning

I am here with you to help you transform psychological predispositions of shame and self-consciousness that keep you from being able to love your own body. The journaling and meditation exercise that follows will help you become more aware, so that you can learn to accept. Let's explore why and how these predispositions manifest in your being and how you can learn to shed and shift them to toward self-love, compassion, healing, and positive affirmations. Be kind to yourself—like you would a small child. Be patient. Healing takes time. I am right here with you. You are not alone.

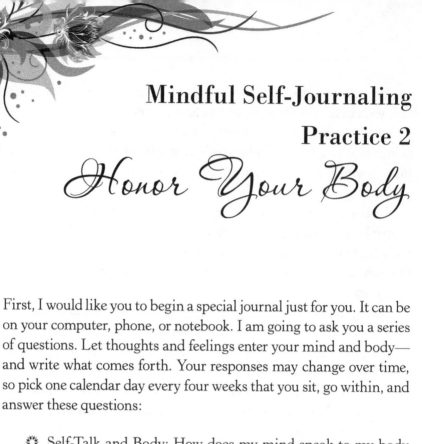

Mindful Self-Journaling
Practice 2
Honor Your Body

First, I would like you to begin a special journal just for you. It can be on your computer, phone, or notebook. I am going to ask you a series of questions. Let thoughts and feelings enter your mind and body—and write what comes forth. Your responses may change over time, so pick one calendar day every four weeks that you sit, go within, and answer these questions:

❋ Self-Talk and Body: How does my mind speak to my body throughout the day? Listen to your thoughts about your own body and about other people's bodies. (How you observe other people's bodies often tells you a lot about how you observe yourself). How do I relate to my body? Am I judgmental of myself? When? Why? How does my body respond to these thoughts? Does my body tense? Does my nervous system quicken? What thoughts about my body help me relax and feel full of relaxed passion? When I look into a mirror, do I tell myself I should look differently than I do? Do I see myself as an object? What do I love about looking at my body? How do I take care of my body? Am I looking at my body as a machine or as something that can help prove my validity? How do I feel about my body? How do I connect with my breath? Where do I put my body? Who do I share my body with? Who do I want to share my body with? How do I touch my own body? What are my feelings around touching my own body? What are my feelings around sharing my body with another? Do I listen to my body? When do I listen to my body? When don't I listen to my body? Do I believe I ought to be given away to others or dissolve my own boundaries to receive the things I think give me value in life? Do I look at my body as a very beautiful creation from the life source through which I can access a spiritual connection to this greater source?

Once you have written down all of your thoughts, apply the same questions to how you see others.

* Physical Health: Try to notice your eating patterns. How do I use food for emotional purposes? What are the emotions I am stuffing down or need soothing from? What foods do I crave? When? Begin to give yourself a daily nutritional intake of necessary proteins, good fats, simple carbohydrates, lots of water, and low caffeine. Try to remove processed sugars, toxins, and heavy flours. See how you feel after you eat certain foods and take notes.

* Physical Fitness: Do you exercise daily? If you do not, ask yourself why? Listen to the many excuses your mind may fabricate. Ask your body what it wants. See where the conflict is. Maybe your mind wants to but energy levels are low.

* Nutritionists, therapists, and trainers are helpful tools in these areas.

* Mindful sleep patterns. Consistency is the key. Be sure to allow yourself a proper amount of rest—but not too much rest. Your body chemistry and mind need to rejuvenate. If you are sluggish and getting ample sleep, you may be depressed or hiding from something emotionally.

✻ Walk outside and spend time in nature. How does my body, heart, and energy respond to fresh air, sunshine, and moonlight? Do I allow myself to gaze at a growing tree or flower? How does my body respond? I would like you to learn to experience with your senses wide open. When you aren't touching or smelling, become amazed. For example, take your time to become enamored drinking in the color and scent of the flower. Reverence or gratitude for beauty and life creates cellular growth on a biological level. Turn your attention to your body. Rejoice in realizing how your body is just as mysterious and profound.

✻ At any age—no matter your current relationship state—imagine that you will be making love at the close of each day and are preparing your temple for optimum sensual expression, pleasure, and mutual exchange. This will raise your libidinal energy levels and make you more aware of how you treat your body.

✻ Daily breathing practice. Slow down and notice your breath at certain points throughout the day. This practice will organically begin to shift your awareness to a healthier mind-set and choices, fewer cravings for heavy foods, and more cravings for self-love, nature, and exercise.

Mantra

I love my body, and I want to listen to all it wants to share with me. I want to listen to my body with compassion and learn to discover all of its hidden wisdom. As I realize the truth of my body, I can come to know the truth of the universe, and trust, not judge, my own healing process.

Mindful Meditation 2
Mind-and-Body Practice

I will guide you through a somatic meditation to help you attune to stimuli and sensation in your body and mind. Practice these focused somatic exercises for about ten minutes three times a week. They will ease tensions and anxieties. You revere source by your choice to attune to your natural rhythm and flow within. As you practice these exercises, like building a muscle, you will learn to mindfully re-attune when you fall into negation of self throughout each day. There are a thousand opportunities throughout the day to get in tune and revive your senses. You can mindfully realize and reconnect at any time. The whole day is a training in sensitivity. Use all of these opportunities to come alive. You learn about yourself most through how your own being responds to the practices—your own relationship to the endeavor. The greatest benefit is the awakening of an inner joy you may have never known.

As days and months of exploring this somatic practice progresses, you may love to try it while standing under your shower in the morning. Or outside. Rest on the beach, feel the sand. Listen to the sounds of the sand. Listen to the sounds of the sea. Go to a tree and touch the tree. Let your fingers traverse the skin of the tree. Touch rock. Feel water, water moves and changes shape, let the movement of the water touch you inside your body because it is touching your outsides.

Now, wherever you are, I invite you to imagine that I am reading this aloud to you. Begin to tune in to your breath. You might wish to revisit the breath practice as a way to warm up and tune in. Think of it as a muscle, and with repetition, you will become spontaneously adjusted to this way of receiving breath and your body.

The eternal vastness of spiritual connection to life force is through your body. Your senses are your doors of perception. Breathe. Allow that channel to open inside of your body. Turn your television off. Turn your music off. For now, gently close your eyes. Listen to what is happening in the room or the space you are in. Even if you don't hear a thing. Listen. There is always something happening. Listen to the resonances in the air. Find the quiet spaces between each thought in your mind. Accept all that you are hearing. Allow all thoughts a gentle acceptance and a fluid morphing, passing. Notice your breath, your expanding diaphragm, pulsing organs, and heart. Feel the movement of vibration in your body, sending breath to the core of each rhythmic pulse. Allow these sensations to affect you inside. The trembling of breath in your body. Take in the sensation of sound, feel how this experience of sound creates a sensory response in your body. Feel where in your body this sensation expands. Your senses connect your internal body and the outside world, outside inside, inside outside, we are in union. Your senses are like receivers for your body. Begin to notice how each sense creates a response within. Taste, touch, smell, listen, breathe. Notice where.

Notice your heart beating. Notice the fire within your heart, the blazing heat, and the sensation. Allow your breath to expand into this internal sensation, the vibrational pulse within. Expanding this body heat, feel your breath in the middle of the sun. As you bring in breath more deeply, notice that you can hear, smell, taste, and feel with a heightened sensation now. Your internal and external sensations are opening up a little bit more now.

I invite into you the earth's vibration, hypnotic hum, and

harmonics. It's happening all the time beneath you, within you. Beyond words, logic, and rational thoughts, listen within for the emotional content these sensations arouse. Allow each sound to shift your internal life.

Now, open your eyes, ears, and nose. Imagine your eyes are like fingertips. See and feel life and beauty in everything everywhere. Let your eyes cast onto whatever is in front of you, the surface of something. Notice all of the facets of the layers of the surface. Like prisms. You might think you only see a white piece of paper, a black computer, or a wooden floor. That surface is made up of thousands of different reflections of color and molecules. They are all made of a vibration of energy that are interlocking to create that surface.

Your skin is created in the same way. Touch the fabric on your body, your skin, your hair. Become enamored. Allow yourself to feel with your eyes, expanding the internal sensations by deepening, expanding your breath into the center of these feelings. Allow yourself to experience any emotions that are aroused. Continue to focus on your breath and internal sensations, moving forward, allowing each moment to build, meld, change, crumble, and build, and on and on.

Notice how willing you are to accept the sensations you are experiencing within. Notice the heat within, the movement of energy. Notice when you begin to block the experience of sensation or feeling. This is simply information about you. Don't judge. Simply bring your awareness back to your breath and continue focusing on taking in the sensation through whichever sense you are focusing on now. This is true intimacy with the outside world. This is the essence of the cultivation of somatic experience in your body and the life-affirming vibrancy of love.

> The moment you accept yourself you become beautiful. When you are delighted with your own body, you will delight others also. Many people will fall in love with you because you, yourself, are in love with yourself. When you are angry with yourself you know that you are ugly, repulsive, horrible. This will repel people, not help them fall in love with you. It will keep them away. Even if they were coming closer to you, the moment they feel your vibration, they will move away. There is no need to chase anybody. The chasing game arises only because we have not been in love with ourselves. Otherwise people come to you. It becomes almost impossible for them not to fall in love with yourself when you are authentically in love with yourself.
>
> —Osho

Chapter 3
Acceptance

In this chapter, we will look at a number of specific terms and practices that are essential for understanding how acceptance can help you heal trauma and create a mind-and-body presence. I will explain what acceptance means, how living in the moment can calm anxiety, and the importance of embracing the unknown. The concepts in this chapter will help you awaken to the present moment, an important step in the healing of trauma and awakening your body-and-mind connection for total awareness. At the close of this chapter, I will offer journaling and meditation practices that will ask you a variety of questions and lead you through practical techniques to teach you how to become present in your mind and body through acceptance and awareness.

Acceptance is a word that I have often heard people pass around: "Just accept what's happening,"

"Get over it—it's all in the past," "Just put it behind you," or "It is what it is!" I invite you to reflect upon how you have heard the word or concept phrased and how it trickles like a stream through your life. I often say, "Grace is a reflection of the spirit hidden within the form. Grace flows from within when you are in a natural receptive space. We cultivate this grace from within by opening up our senses."

Understanding True Acceptance

Through accepting the experience of all that is happening in and around you—all that you are receiving—you become present to the moment. Your body is a great big receiver. We can receive most deeply, melting defenses, by practicing this kind of mind-body acceptance.

Acceptance is considered a simple concept, but it can be extremely difficult to put into action. To sit down, breathe, and accept what is happening in the present moment, you may first need to ward off the part of you that is fighting against accepting what is. This part of you doesn't want to feel at all. Instead, it wants action toward immediate change. This is a defensive measure. A self-protective part of you wants to survive, and it is a necessary, valuable aspect of the self.

This self-protective part of you aims for survival, and it needs to understand that you can—and eventually will—choose to take actions to change uncomfortable circumstances. If you don't know what action to take, life will organically and inevitably create change for you. Change is the only thing we can truly depend on. However, it seems to be a law of nature that change or transformation can only happen synchronously after settling into the full presence of what is. The most organic change occurs when we first find a place of contained wholeness. In this space, pressure is lifted—and transformation is free to happen in a natural way. Practice acceptance of what is. This doesn't mean passivity and denial.

I know this isn't easy all the time, but let's try to cultivate the awareness like one would a muscle in the body. It eventually becomes life a reflexive response. The first action to take in any circumstance is to breathe and to feel. Let's try to see the situation, whatever it may be, with open-minded curiosity. Let's become so curious that instead of shutting down, we seek to accept our many feelings and perspectives. Seek to see the circumstance for its many parts, complexities, realities, and truth.

Stillness within occurs when we first accept the truth of what is. Try it right now. Anxiety decreases when we accept what is happening right now in our minds and bodies. You see? While positive self-talk is an important shift to cultivate, the importance of accepting negativity—or not-so-pleasurable parts of our daily existence—is a path toward transcendence. Negativity, or the perception that something is negative, is part of life. The moment we allow ourselves to accept the negative experience, or the darkness as some call it, we open to new perspectives. We are not stuck in anxiety and defense, and we can begin to find new ways of perceiving and perhaps solving the circumstance.

Spiritual Bypass

Some people think it is important to banish all negative feelings and talk ourselves out of it through affirmations, positive self-talk, and meditation. I call this a spiritual bypass. This route in my experience only causes more separation between mind and body. It is like telling a child who had a bad dream that the dream didn't really happen and to ignore the feelings. It's like saying light is the opposite of darkness.

I am saying that light and darkness—or the perceptions thereof— are like our concept of time-space continuum and chaos theory. You cannot have total awareness without allowing yourself to be present to all that is happening now. Good or bad. Pleasurable or non-pleasurable. In fact, perhaps there is no reality to the good or bad judgments. Perhaps this is all an appearance or fabrication of your mind. Perhaps you can accept that you really have no concept of what is happening in your energetic vibration. Trust that all is as it needs to be, trusting in source as moving toward synchronicity for your greater healing at all times—even when it makes no mental sense to you. Healing, awareness, and transcendence are found when we accept all that is now.

A dear friend said, "Yes. The sky is clear. It only appears to be blue, gray, red, black, or white at any given moment. The mind is the sky: limitless. We may want to stop trying to measure it."

Notice, Reflect, and Observe

How about you? Have you already had a really busy day? Maybe you had a lot going on at work, hit some traffic, or found yourself sandwiched on a busy subway. Maybe your stocks were down a huge percentage—or you didn't have enough change in your pocket to get breakfast. No matter where you are or who you are, there are going to be moments and circumstances in each day that you find yourself fighting against the tide. Notice, reflect, and observe. At what points in this day did you get stuck in a moment of negating the circumstance?

Maybe you were fighting against the traffic and thinking, *Oh, this is so stupid. I shouldn't be sitting in traffic. I can't believe these people drive so stupidly. I could be doing something better with my time.* Maybe you were at work and thinking, *Oh, this job isn't good enough for me, I should be doing something better with my time. I should be off on an exotic island somewhere.* Maybe someone said something you didn't like and you thought, *Oh, gosh. Why do I know people like this? How could I change who they are to better suit my needs? What could I say to make them see things the way that I do?*

In these moments, you may have started to drift, daydream, or fantasize. You might have fallen into a rut of aggression as a way to negate experiencing the moment. You might notice that when you engage in negating or pushing away reality with obsessive wishes and thoughts for something different, your body physically hardens and moves into shutting down. This is because negating your open living experience creates pressure, tension, and anxiety. This stops the flow of energy transformation in your being.

When you engage in accepting and experiencing what is, your body is given space to open. Your mind and body can find a calm, serene acceptance. This gives you space to listen within and make clear choices for actions.

Negating often leads one's mind to believe it is doing something helpful by going into action to create change, but this action is most often a reactive response rather than a choice. Of course, there are extremely dangerous situations when the fight-or-flight response is instinctual and most helpful. Here, I am talking about situations where we think we must go into fight-or-flight mode to fix something right away, but we need to engage in acceptance and special, thoughtful attention so that we may gather more information, choosing action mindfully, or at least taking the time to do so. Sometimes simply letting go and placing your trust in organic change is the best response.

While this fight-or-flight response to discomfort and frustration may be a defense motivated by a wish to survive, this fear-based response often leads to more negative experiences or anxiety. Things may blow up and cause you to have to stop altogether and reconfigure what is going on because you've run your train into a brick wall. The circumstances around you are falling apart.

Let's build the foundation of our lives on a clear channel grounded in the truth of our experiences rather than in defensive, reactive fear. After all, life is energy that needs to transform. As much as chaos transforms, acceptance of circumstances can ease the pressures that create explosion, diffuse, and open you to new, more sustainable growth experiences.

The sun does remain in a state of perfectly synchronized explosion as its means for growth and survival, but as humans, we can easily overwhelm and spontaneously combust. Accepting that integration and disintegration are happening in and around us all the time will help us feel less pressure and find moments of synchronized stillness more easily.

The Acceptance Paradox

A paradox of mindful living is that to allow organic change in any situation, you must first accept it the way it is. Accepting something doesn't mean you have to agree with it or like it. Acceptance is about letting go of the judgmental ego and releasing the tension of negative energy surrounding a situation. In order to move forward, we must make peace with what we are experiencing and let go of any willful attachments to desired outcomes.

Do not deny anything—this transforms everything. Accept whatever you are. You are a great energy of many multidimensional energies. Accept it and move with every energy. With deep sensitivity. With awareness. With love. With understanding. Move with it. Let it live inside of your body. Then every wish become energy, and every energy becomes healing.

One of the most healing and transformative forces in the universe and humanity is the fact that we are all interconnected. Living beings are all interconnected through vibration. That vibration creates and is within every single other living, vibrating thing around us. This mystery is our reality. Think about it. Simply by waking up in the morning and living your life, you are choosing to exist in pure acceptance of this absolute unknown. Without thinking about it, you rise, you wash, you nourish, you create, you work, you commune, and you sleep. Somehow, you accept that you, we, are in this life.

There may be moments for each of us, when we fall into existential questioning: Why am I here? What are the origins of life? What is the purpose of life? At some point, we let it go, unanswered, and simply chose to accept that we are here for some reason and went back to the flow. We meld back into living with our best ability, engaging in this cataclysmic energy of change that we have no real control over, and without thinking for the most part, we adapt to what naturally occurs.

Nothing in this universe remains static. Life isn't meant to be permanent. It is meant to be experienced. A calm, serene, and spiritually connected perspective is born through the acceptance and reverence for the unknown.

Ah, breath. Let us become curious rather than afraid. All we have power over is our perspective and our actions.

The Unknown

We must examine our relationship to the unknown. Let us practice a conscious awareness that there is much we do not know, and that we will never know, followed by conscious acceptance of this. Ask yourself, "What do these concepts mean to me? How does accepting this affect my body, my mind, and my awareness?" Deep acceptance of these concepts may be jarring at first, but coupled by a faith in organic synchronicity, it will lead to a deep level of serenity within your core.

Acceptance asks you to trust in the organizational pattern of life. We can have an idea of where we are going circumstantially—based on an outline of what we have planned and our trust in our own free will—but we have no idea where we came from, how we were given these flowers to smell or air to breathe, or what the true magic or mystery is behind it. We are asked to accept that we have no true factual knowledge of, or ability to predict, exactly what is going to or ought to happen next.

We can begin to learn to look into and beyond our organic matter. Start to revere the possibility of tuning into the many vast aspects of self and universe within and around us. At every moment, there is inevitable change. This means that we are truly spontaneous. We have limitless potential. We are energy. What we can do is accept and live in wonder and awe of all that.

Mantra

I am completely living within the mystery of this life force. I am a part of this organizational, energetic pattern of life. I am consciously remaining attuned to my body's resonance, seeking to listen to my heart and my intuitive wisdom. I live in observance of my life's patterns as they emerge. I seek to trust that the right things for my greatest soul transformation and healing are unfolding for my own, unique path.

Pitfalls of Society and Media

Unfortunately, if we turn on the TV, for example, we often get messages we perceive as telling us that we are not good enough. Maybe the words or messages aren't so blatant, but the images we see may cause our minds to perceive that we must live up to a certain standard to be of value. We may hear or see text that plays with our mind, dangling a carrot that tells us what we ought to be thinking about, ought to find morally or socially important to our lives, ought to look like, or ought to want to experience. We may be motivated by this and strive to succeed at the creation of these images. Motivation through comparison or competition may drive us toward the achievement of things we are told we must have to enjoy a happy, well-respected life. This is real motivation and is connected to the life instinct.

Motivation

Let's analyze where our motivation comes from. If it is spawned from competition or comparison, it is often coming from the fear that we are not worthy of existence or are overwhelmed by our own powerlessness. We want to bypass these existential questions and have answers to all that is unknown, thus proving our worth in this world. It is a blatant misconception to think that once we achieve everything to the standard and mark that our social mores, television, and the media tell us is the right way to be, we will have achieved happiness and fulfillment. All that really comes of this pursuit is that we believe that we ought to be different than we are, try to deny what we are or what we feel, and end up dividing ourselves from our souls and box ourselves into a state of compartmentalized living.

Internal Rejection

As we mature into adults, it is imperative that we learn to handle our impulses in a responsible way. How do we do this? An aspect of maturation is learning to withstand frustration. Learning to withstand frustration, accept what is, and make rational choices are all important to development. Otherwise, we would be like children, darting off in all directions without thinking, impulsively, but there are two sides.

Withstanding frustration toward maturation means we learn to take certain actions that we may not want to because we are seeking to reach a higher goal. We keep focused on the process as it unfolds, with the bigger goal in mind. This is important.

However, much of the time, what happens within this great depth of contained impulses and control of focus is that we separate vastly from our internal selves. We aren't taught to integrate our deep essence, inner truth, into the moments as they unfold. We often get caught up in a world of tasking and grinding toward a goal that we believe will make us more valuable to the world at large, but we haven't taken the time to get in touch with what truly motivates us, the fulfillment of passion. This happens because much of our societal upbringing is based on behavior modifications and rewards for best behavior according to the higher-ups. Often, shaming takes precedence if we differ from the received code of ethics set in place by the patriarchal system. Hence, we learn to negate our inner essence, inner childlike curiosity, and spontaneity of thought.

During these moments of internal rejection, rejecting our true selves, we tell ourselves that our essential selves hold no value. We create a life that isn't vital. We are not growing and transforming organically and freely because we aren't fully attuned to our internal vibration or pulse. When goals aren't born from true passion and are chosen for accolades and acceptance by others—when we are taught and choose to live by social rules and status quo values—we don't feel connected to the things that are happening in our lives. We don't truly feel aligned with the goals we have set in place. We place no value or trust in learning about our own selves and hearts. We travel down this path of separation from our true self, our true nature. Our deeper, inner longings become quite mysterious and are rendered meaningless, lost, or forgotten.

You can begin to trust in cultivating an awareness of the feelings that come up for you by accepting and valuing your true self. These aspects of self are of value because this where your vitality is bred. The more aligned you seek to be with your soul calling, your true self, the more this spontaneous wellspring of life that exists within your mind and body can organically prosper.

You have a choice. Begin to find stillness in your life. Listen deeply to your intentions and wishes—and then accept and explore these aspects as valuable pieces of information about yourself and your inner life. Identify the internalized rules and messages that have affected you. Accept these learned behaviors. As you accept and analyze, you can begin to choose whether, which, and how you want to take beliefs and goals on as your own. Here, you move away from idealizing a better way to live, and into exploration and even fascination with what is, with your true self. This is awareness.

Even when whatever it is feels like a thorn in your side, seeking to get away from the circumstances that are bothering you rather than first settling into accepting they are there, stops you from experiencing the truth of what you feel—what your heart and intuitive self are communicating to you. Of course, you have the choice to change, but authentic change and awareness occur when the action comes from acceptance in an organic space rather than one reacting out of defense against the truth of what is.

Listening to the part of yourself that is saying, "Hey, I have a longing to explore this," "I feel this way," or "I fear this" doesn't mean you will actually throw everything away and go after change impulsively. It means you are valuing all of yourself and introspectively seeking to accept and know and understand more about yourself—or else you can choose to tell yourself to be quiet or that you are not important.

In this quiet space, as you continue on this path, you can begin to receive, explore, and perceive with curiosity the circumstances in your life as an opportunity. How is this circumstance serving me as a teacher?

Expand and shift your vibration by learning to attune to and rest into your experiences with acceptance. In this, you become more aware of yourself and your energetic patterns, and you gain greater

breadth of choice. In this space, you can begin to authentically transmute and transform.

Only in quiet waters do things present themselves as undistorted.
Only in a quiet mind is perception of the world effectively illuminated.
Life is meant to be adored. The more synchronicities you experience
in your life, the more you know you are aligned and listening to your
true resonance, thus following the path of your soul-led vibration.

You will see an example of this in your body and mind when
you study how accepting helps you become one with your emotions.
Notice how you feel about something, even if you are really angry,
really sad, really in love, or really excited. When you sit with your
feelings as they are without going into action and learn to tune in to
the somatic response and movement of energy in your body, the feelings and perceptions in your mind will shift, change, and transform
naturally.

Choices come through accepting the truth of what is happening
in your body in accordance with the circumstance being presented
in your life. Suppose you are sitting in your car, falling into a rut or
mind-set of negating the present moment, and saying, "Oh, this is
so annoying. I'm sitting here in traffic, and I could be at the beach. I
should be at the beach. I should have a better life. This shouldn't be
happening to me." (Uh-oh, you are shoulding on yourself.)

Accept that you don't have control and can't change the circumstance. You can drop into body and emotional awareness, truly being
with and experiencing life. As you drop into acceptance and experience what is, you will viscerally shift into a calming of tension,
anxiety, and pressure. You are literally letting go of the energy it takes
to negate a circumstance. It requires a lot of pressure from the mind
against the body to negate or defend against a feeling. This only creates tension, anxiety, and a quick response to take action to feel better.
The moment you drop into acceptance and feeling, you will open to
becoming fluid and sending messages to your body that it is okay to
be you and that you are of value. In this place of acceptance, you can
attune to what occurs next. Perhaps you will suddenly feel inspired to
stop "shoulding," put on a favorite song, or become filled with a new

idea for resolving an issue at work. Acceptance allows us unlimited potential for growth.

Your mind can get stuck on remembering and planning. Reflection on the past and planning the future are essential to our progression in life. The challenge is to not live in the past or future. We can reflect, but it is dangerous to get stuck there. This can become problematic since it almost always results in multiple expressions of fear and anxiety.

All too often, we keep our emotional pain alive by replaying and magnifying our hurts in our minds. It's as if by experiencing our painful memories again, we unconsciously wish this will somehow change the past, but that can never happen, and it often causes unnecessary suffering. Generally, this repetition of thought and memory is a sign that your body wants to feel better and your mind is seeking clarification as to how, but often it occurs in a defended state of reliving and defending rather than curiously exploring the healing your soul is seeking. For many of us, in a twisted way, we may unconsciously be drawn to the mental excitement and drama of replaying. Perhaps we use it to gain sympathy from others or as a distraction from deeper, visceral truths. Whatever the reason, we can become drawn to pain like a moth to a flame.

I simply remind you: Cry wholly—and let go. Forgive fully—and let go. Live expansively—and let go. Laugh wholeheartedly—and let go. Love deeply—and let go.

Begin to notice when you are going through the motions or defending against being, and if so, accept this. Here, life can continue to evolve. New thoughts and feelings can occur. It begins with acceptance of what is now.

Presence is more rewarding than the busy-bee mentality. Let's not mistake productivity with being busy. They are not the same. It seems many are more busy than productive these days. Being effective is better than being simply productive. Being present gives you the opportunity to be effective. Don't get me wrong. I too enjoy the feeling of being productive! It is exhilaration, forward movement, and evolution. However, just like everything else, the importance of goal completion, finishing tasks, and productivity can become magnified to the point where our achievements, our finances, and our ability to bring something to the table are used to measure our worth as human beings! We, in turn, begin to measure our worth and self-satisfaction through the same lens we use to find happiness. Seek to be grounded and effective with your measures rather than just listlessly productive.

Why hurry through life? Taking the time to focus and become present is the difference between being effective, motivated, and inspired and merely productive.

Acceptance and Life Force

Libidinal or sensual feelings in our bodies are happening all day long. Nobody can deny them! Sexuality is the core of our life force nature. It is our survival instinct to meld, bond, and create. Maybe we don't have a driving force to connect with another person all the time, but sensual and sexual feelings and fantasies are happening in our bodies all day long. Try to observe this experience in you now. Maybe you feel a sensual wave of energy in your body when you breathe. Maybe you see something pleasing to the eye, something that reminds you of a sensual experience that you have had, and this brings a wave of pleasure to your body simply for the pleasure it arouses in your fantasy life.

Your natural spirit of intention is to synchronize, procreate, and manifest. The foundational instinct we have as beings is to live and grow. The more aware we can become of our sexuality and our sexual feelings inside our bodies, the more vastly we allow ourselves to feel fluid. When we accept these aspects of self, we aren't as likely to be driven to act, act out, or become victims or perpetrators of aggression. When we allow ourselves to experience our feelings or our bodies' sensory experiences throughout the day, we are able to hear our intuitive essential selves and accept our internal circumstances without defending or denying.

We don't want to be predators or desperate for attention. In acceptance of self, we can experience our bodies' energy without needing to act on defending against it. When we deny the feelings, they become dangerous.

Identify the feelings, accept them, contain the desires, and become conscious of our actions. As we know, sexuality is very repressed and shamed in society. The subject is vast, and each person has their own path healing this. We also all know that people who unconsciously or aggressively act out their desires or shames or self-hatred on others or themselves are very harmful for this society and need to be healed. We do not want to become aggressors or victims. Acceptance of the feelings in our bodies can cultivate conscious choice around what to do with these feelings. This is a huge subject, and it deserves deep respect and sensitivity.

As healthy beings, the more we allow these feelings in our bodies to circulate and live within us, the more vital and healthy we feel, and energetically alive we become every day.

We are talking a lot about acceptance: all you taste, touch, smell, see, feel. This allowance of self will make you feel kinder and more open-hearted toward others. Accepting where you are now allows you to open to noticing all the beauty that surrounds you in the present moment of every single day. Melting

> Only through total acceptance can you grow. Then use every energy you have. How can you use them? Accept them. Then find out what these energies are. The more you try to negate the bigger it becomes. The more attractive it becomes. The more you try to negate it, the more you feel invited. You cannot negate it. Yet this tendency to negate and destroy, destroys the mind. It destroys the awareness and the sensitivity that can understand it. Only a deep sensitivity can understand anything. Only a deep feeling, a deep moving into it, can understand anything. Somehow you have to go out of the garden. Then how can you be aware?
> —Osho

defenses and negations, you will have more gratitude for living. Here, joyful moments turn into the next moment.

Be easy on yourself. It is natural to have emotional responses to somatic experience. This is life. Our minds often try to take us into the past or worry about the future. The moment you try to clamp down or control or negate your feelings, you lose admission to life force potential that would lead to your natural transformation and higher consciousness. We have no concept of exactly what that could be. Potential is limitless. Life force is limitless. Continue to practice tuning in to the present moment. Join me as we tune in to learn some acceptance journaling and mind-and-body practices!

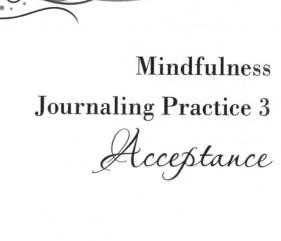

Mindfulness
Journaling Practice 3
Acceptance

Through this journaling practice, we seek to uncover desires that we may have been pushing away. Intentions you have that you didn't know you really had. Wishes you have been ignoring. Perhaps a desire you have but tell yourself is stupid. We want to listen inwardly and accept our internal world. We want to know ourselves better. Everything you have an intention toward doing is valuable to accept and explore internally, not necessarily to decide to do. That would be impulsive if you just jumped into anything and everything, as a child does. Children are very in touch with their intentions, impulses, instincts, wants, and needs. As adults, we deserve to hear ourselves, the spontaneous, alive desires within. We can only then move through the world in a state of introspective awareness, make free choices for self-expression, and create the potential to fulfill our deepest heart-led longings and intentions.

Journal these questions for about ten minutes a few times a week. Begin to ask yourself these questions as a way to check in emotionally:

What am I feeling right now? What am I drawn to doing or feeling right now? What am I truly passionate about? What am I afraid to feel? To explore? What am I inspired to feel or explore? Are there feelings or desires I want to say out loud? What creative forces inside of me or thoughts do I want to share with others or myself? Recognize these as communications within you that are valuable! Are there thoughts or feelings you want to say to another person but have been holding back? Are there conversations you have been shying away from? Why? Don't feel it will do any good? Think it's stupid? Do feelings really not matter? Which of my senses do I gravitate toward most? Do I love sound vibrations? Smells? Touching fabrics, skin, or metal? Do I like cool sensations or warm ones? Fuzzy or coarse? Prickly. These are just examples. Ask yourself what you like to sense. Notice this in yourself throughout the day. Notice where your mind goes when you daydream or fantasize. Notice what you continuously return to. This will change on different days, months, or years of your life. These longings act as information from you to you, about you. Accept and explore.

Mindfulness Acceptance
Practice 3
Soul Consciousness Meditation

A good way to begin this process of self-discovery is to sit quietly in meditation and imagine your awareness reaching out. Imagine your awareness expanding far and wide into the world around you. See yourself attuning to the rhythms of life and putting forth energy that will attract many new opportunities for growth. Every aspect of your life seems magical and sacred when you open your mind and expand your awareness to the world around you. See yourself as a divine creature, god, or goddess. Listen to where you feel you would direct your energies if aligned with these aspects of self. Imagine yourself transcending negative repetitions. Feel how that is in your body. Imagine what your life looks like if you make choices to lead you toward vibrational light and light rather than fear-based material repetitions on this earth. Feel the light of universe in your heart. Feel the power to manifest anything you envision. Feel your soul calling in your visceral being, cells, veins, and heart. How does your heart feel when you imagine yourself fulfilling some destiny or true calling? How are you affecting the universe and the world around you through this manifestation of light and soul-consciousness from your being? When you re-enter your

daily life, try to access these visions and aspects of yourself, the god and goddess in your consciousness. They are there. You are divine. Try to actively communicate and manifest from this place.

Chapter 4

The Biology of Love

In this chapter, we will discuss how healthy love and pleasure-seeking can help relieve the negative effects of trauma. I will explain the evolution of love, the effects of love attained and denied on your mind and body, fear and gluttony, and self-destructive pleasures versus healthy pleasures. These concepts are core elements for the foundational healing of trauma, awakening the body-and-mind connection, and developing an understanding of the benefits of learning to allow love into your life. At the close of this chapter, journaling and meditation practices will help you understand the positive relationship to love, touch, and the mind-and-body union.

Humans depend on love. Love is intrinsic to the history of evolution and the basis for human society. You can feel it in your own body now. The biology of love is cellular, visceral, and physiological, and it stems from a deeply rooted, primitive need for survival. It is grounded in a powerful yearning for connection.

Very often, we feel like we are not deserving of love. This feeling is particularly prevalent among those who struggle with trauma, addiction, or anxiety. Healing and rejuvenating teach us that we are worthy of being loved and open to accepting love from those around us and giving love in return. This will help you be successful on the path to wellness.

> The planet does not need more successful people. The planet desperately needs more peacemakers, healers, restorers, storytellers and lovers of all kinds.
> —Dalai Lama

Nature

Let's observe all organic matter: insects, birds, fish, mammals, plants, trees, and other forms of life on earth. We see this consistent movement toward connection, bonding. This striving for union to sustain and develop life is not unique to our human species; it is an inherent dynamic in every creature's ability to survive.

Humans have a longer period of infancy than other mammals, and we need to communicate through a progression of emotional stages as we mature. These stages give rise to a hierarchy of desires, fantasies, needs, and developmental milestones.

Love is a quality of emotion and a bioelectric current of energy. This powerful, unconscious drive and conscious emotion is the fundamental celebration in literature and religion. In the spiritual sense, love is considered the noblest human experience. Learning to generate, give, and receive the resonance of love is the foundation of all therapeutic healing practices because the experience of love creates a deep healing chemistry. We are driven to seek the experience of love to survive. We get this feeling from spiritual realms, intimate communications, and sexual bonding.

Humans also have the instinct to make love year-round. Our females are active sexually year-round and have the ability for multiple orgasms. Humans spend more time in the lovemaking act than other species. For humans, lovemaking is not just used for procreative purposes; it is an act of emotional bonding. Lovemaking is a way to experience psychological, internal longings, and this creates multiple layers of emotional experiences, such as yearning, frustration, and connection. This requires communication. Because humans experience complex feelings and behaviors, the avenues through which humans seek bonding are highly developed. Love and lovemaking can also feel quite confusing for those who have experienced trauma.

Quest for Union

Love is a quest for the union with sensual objects that we experienced as infants (primary care) and for a communion with absolute power or source. Throughout life, we consciously and unconsciously seek our ideal of perfect love, truth, and protection. No matter what we experienced after birth, almost all of us believe that we once had this ultimate union and continually envision regaining that experience. However, throughout the journey of our maturing lives, each of us meets unique challenges that shape the emotional capacity to give and receive love, which affects the body's openness to the flow of love's energy. We each develop unique closure and opening habits in response to our specific life challenges. Yet, inherently, unconsciously, and consciously—at the core of all we do and are in this life—we are drawn into this golden circle. It is a constant quest for a euphoric state of being.

In the earliest period of life, each human experiences a deep dependency and a rich inner life. This is when a child's complex human character starts to take shape. The infant—etymologically, the one who cannot speak—lives in a world of images, desires, and great pleasures. Freud would say this early infantile sensuality is the beginning of a polymorphous erotic adventure and is mostly comprised of primitive bodily wants and desires. Freud said, "Giants loom over us, seemingly capable of satisfying all wants. They represent Eden, a world of perfection."

However, gaps open and burst the container of pure bliss when Mother is distracted or Father fails some test of protection. They are human and not necessarily bad parents. Like all paradise, this one of the infant ebbs and flows and is lost and regained over and over again. As the experience of these gaps begins to imprint on the psyche between the moments of desire and gratification, the mind fills them with fantasy, wishes, yearning, and resentment, as forms of self-soothing or survival mechanisms. The toddler will never give up a wish to satisfy libidinal yearning, and as we mature into adulthood, this longing drives us, manipulates us, dissatisfies us, and ultimately fuels an instinct to remain in existence, striving to restore this libidi-nal bliss through dreams and fantasy. We seek and dream. We dream of perfect authority and love, frequently circling from romance to disillusionment and back again.

In Freud's *Infantile Sexuality* (1910), he observed that romantic love inevitably circles back and forth from romance to disillusionment. Often this cycle occurs within the same couple—if both people in the partnership are willing to remain committed to working through the humilities and humiliations the attachment calls forth. This creates a flow of dilemma and longings, a progression toward equanimity, poise. These frustrations, as Freud puts it, are part of the organic flow of life. We must learn to trust that they are signposts on the way to spiritual and emotional growth.

Philip Reiff's *The Mind of the Moralist* (1979) suggests that there is something Eastern in this Freudian ethos. The quest for equanim-ity in psychoanalysis is akin to Buddhist attempts to attain emotional and spiritual calm through yoga and meditation. The yogic seeker is hoping to feel absolute completion through a melding with spirit. The many phases they experience, the frustrations and highs they must en-dure, are one and the same as the human commitment to partnership and attachment arouses.

Ultimately, the motivation to sustain our survival drives our spe-cies. The most adaptive development in the foundations of our evolu-tion seems to have been born from our great human capacity for love and loving. It is believed that because humans are innately aware that we need love to be able to survive, and because our maturation time is lengthened, and because this quest for the attainment of love from one source or another is often circuitous and frustrating, that the human's brain created a more highly developed potential for this conscious and caring connectivity we call love.

We alone have the ability to communicate with language. Language allows us the possibility of lengthened, shared physical and emotional interaction because language allows us to express internal feelings. Language gives us the vehicle to be able to communicate emotions that help us understand one another's needs. This gives us the possibility for a deeper intimacy because it leads us toward empathy. Empathy allows us greater satisfaction through deeper connection or union.

Taking It In

Isn't it truly awesome that this libidinal force, this inexplicable force of nature that somehow bonds all living things together, is so very silently wise? Driven by the organic desire and need to reach deeper levels of intimacy, to enhance union, connectivity, balance, and ultimately synchronicity, the human mind and body evolved toward language. Today, humans are born with the cerebral ability to create, memorize, and contextualize language. No other living form has capabilities this complex.

Is the emotion of love a striving for connection or oneness with another? Is spirituality a striving for union or oneness with what we call the divine? Are these all linked as one and the same? Do we seek to find the divine in the other, through human connection?

We may have been taught that we only find the divine in spiritual practices defined by religions, that sensuality and emotion, though each a quest for connection and union, are different or even lower forms of connection. Are they?

Love and Trauma

The ability to freely give and receive love is fragile. Traumatic experiences can all too easily dent or damage your retained experience of love as a blissful state of sharing. Because you have experienced a traumatic experience, you have learned that people are also capable of great acts of cruelty. A part of your mind may have decided to ensure that you will never be hurt again. Without even realizing it, you may have decided—or your mind will try to protect you from future cruelty—that people, no matter how loving they may be toward you, are dangerous. This assumption results in you leaning toward mistrust, avoiding vulnerability, and shying away from emotional intimacy.

Shying away from emotional intimacy can manifest in the form of shying away from physical and emotional relationships. It can also appear in the opposite way. Some who have been sexually, physically, emotionally traumatized may engage in high levels of sex but keep their hearts untouchable. Some may even appear to have relations with many people, like polyamory, but remain emotionally distant from all. Some may even engage in marriages but always keep a part of their emotional and physical selves on reserve, unable to give in to a full companionship or mutual trusting bond with another human being.

Recovering Your Willingness to Love and Be Loved

It is possible to resolve and heal trauma. Sometimes this trauma is known, but it is often unknown or blocked. First, we need to excavate the wounds slowly, in our own time. Working with a good therapist who understands trauma can be a safe way to heal because you aren't alone with the terrifying memories and feelings. In this relationship, you also learn to receive love and care from a consistent, outside source, in a contained and safe environment. As you allow yourself to move more deeply into healing, your physical, mental, and emotional knots begin to relax. This is a good beginning. Once the wounds begin resolving, space is created for something new to emerge. At this point in the journey, you will find yourself open to giving and receiving love. Bringing love to trauma is a sacred moment that affects your current relationships, releases the generations that preceded your life, and allows health to enter the generations that follow you. There is a natural progression and flow between trauma and love that has extraordinary potential. You can begin to allow the vital force of love that is within you and around you all the time to enter, but can you allow yourself to receive it fully?

Again, learning how to be loved is a vital part of your healing. Part of learning how to be loved again is learning how to interact with people who express kindness, care, concern, nurture, and attention and expressing these feelings and intentions toward your own self and being. However, many trauma survivors relive childhood experiences with unresponsive or abusive partners. This often happens without seeing the reasons why because beneath awareness is a repetition toward unresolved trauma, coupled by a wish to resolve it and make things right. Childhood wounds cannot be repaired. You must become aware of these repetitions and work on changing those cycles to save you from entering a cycle of abuse.

Here are a few things to think about as you regain your ability to accept someone's care, concern, and nurturing. Walking through this recovery process with a therapist's help is very helpful. You will benefit from learning to trust carefully chosen outside help.

✦ Observe yourself and your child within. Recognize what triggers your trauma feelings.

✦ Slow down or step back when feelings escalate to assess if you are in an abusive situation or are projecting abuse due to fear of intimacy and vulnerability.

✦ Work with yourself to stay grounded and in tune with your body and emotions as much as possible. You want to develop trust with yourself first and foremost.

✦ Try to allow yourself to ask someone for help or support.

✦ Notice when you are pulling back emotionally or physically and ask yourself what is happening in and around you that may have caused this response.

✦ Begin to understand when your emotional responses are out of proportion to the circumstance and spend time with yourself and your inner child to understand what you are feeling.

✦ Take time for self-care and learn to allow pleasure to enter your body and mind.

The Evolution of Pleasure

Scientists and researchers have begun to look at the role of pleasure in human survival. During the course of evolution, nature has presented chemical rewards that provide our bodies with enormous pleasure. These chemicals are especially present when we are loved and are loving toward others. At the root of all libidinal drive is pleasure. It is a quest for pleasure that drives us to seek love, the powerful conduit to human sustenance.

Scientists have found that the most successful (often synthetic) chemicals (or neuroreceptor stimulants) in the treatment of mental illnesses have biological similarities to the organic chemicals that the body and mind create naturally when we are engaging in all three forms of connection: sensual connection, emotional connection, and spiritual union with a source, whatever that means to you individually. Due to the discovery of these responses to certain chemicals, and the body's natural ability to create these chemicals when engaging in union, scientists have observed that these three forms of union derive from a deep, cellular, visceral, physiological human experience that is fundamentally rooted in the innate need for pleasure.

The natural chemical endorphin (endogenous morphine) is an opiate that masks pain and provides extra energy in the body by calming the nervous system. Endorphins are the first thing your body creates when a wound, pain, or injury occurs. Let's think about a more primitive time in history, before the human species, language, emotional bonding, and intimacy had evolved. Have you ever observed an animal licking another wounded animal or licking its own wounds? This is a loving acting of soothing to help heal the pain or incision by sanitizing, touching, and giving the other, or self, a sense of both male and female attributes: being held and contained and also being protected and defended. Once the nervous system is calmed, the body has the capacity for greater blood circulation, oxygenation, and the creation of other chemicals that promote healing or energize action.

When humans are in pain, the act of being touched in a caring way (soothing) will promote the greater production of endorphins in the body. Giving the body the necessary chemicals needed to numb the pain and energize the body toward healing is driven by an innate or unconscious wisdom toward balance, synchronicity, and repair. Often, when in crisis, touch is spontaneously expressed through visceral, energetic movements in the body. This also happens naturally when people are feeling strong resonances of love. In these moments of felt mutual resonance, the nervous system calms and heart expansion occurs. Less fear and less need to separate and flee instills a feeling of pleasure. These pleasure-inducing chemicals sustain bonding through the expression of attunement, the give and take of intimacy and empathy, and life-affirming connections with others.

The experience of falling in love and the intense pleasures of sensual and spiritual love are infused with a rush of chemical rewards, rising levels of chemicals like phenylethylamine (an amphetamine-like substance), endorphins, oxytocin, and serotonin—that most likely explain the euphoric high of magnanimous heart expansion, intuitive consciousness, and spiritual energy. This mutual resonance is much like what an infant may experience in the womb or in the first few years of bonding with a primary caretaker. When all needs and desires are fulfilled by the other, synchronicity is achieved. We are naturally transported to a euphoric bliss through a shared feeling of warmth and safety. This paradise is what we desire when longing for sensual and spiritual union. Mystics of old have described their experiences in the language of sensuality. In the midst of sensual passion and spiritual illumination is the poetry of love.

When we experience this endless sense of calm and energy for a sustained period, we are ultimately transported to a meditative, spiritual, or trancelike state that involves chains in the electrical activity of the brain, recognized as altered consciousness. This transcendence creates powerful changes in our sense of time, space, identity, emotional state, and motor output.

Orgasm has been greatly used to induce mystical states because orgasm is recognized as an altered state of consciousness, including changes in sense of time, space, identity, strong emotions, and great changes in motor output. Shared orgasm, the giving of touch and pleasure, the trance—even if experienced for a moment in time—feels like we have entered a vast pool of warmth, have been soothed and calmed, tended to, rejuvenated in a way beyond what we could have consciously fathomed, ultimately fully accepted, felt, and contained for a moment.

We seek love, and pleasure is at its core. At the root of all love seeking and thus survival is pleasure. Humans, in sensual bonding, emotional love, and spiritual union, experience the chemicals that take away pain, heal wounds, create energy, and give us a feeling of profound connection and euphoric bliss. It is pleasure we seek for survival, and it brings us an ultimate high when achieved organically.

Love Attained and Love Denied

There is a cost if we don't receive or accept the importance of love in our lives. Neglect can include physical neglect (not providing food, clothing, shelter), emotional neglect (not providing love, comfort, or affection), and medical neglect (not providing needed medical care). Verbal abuse can harm a person's self-worth or emotional well-being. Many people who are being neglected or abused abstain from telling anyone because they are afraid of being abandoned, blamed, or not believed. The long-term effects of neglect and abuse can be a lowered capacity to cope with stress and anxiety, self-harm and neglect, a wish to run away from all attachments and intimacies, and an inability to realize dreams and desires. These effects can manifest in a child who has been neglected or abused or an adult who is in a neglectful or abusive relationship. Ultimately, the long-term and short-term effects of love denied, either by your partners, parents or self, and love that you deny from people who are trying to give it to you, are vast. Healing from neglect and abuse and allowing love, support, and pleasure into your life and being are vital for your survival.

Fear and Gluttony

Conversely, there is another side to the seeking of love and pleasure. If pleasure is a yearning intertwined with our need to survive, and this creation of loving bonding increases health in our cells and bodies, why is seeking pleasure for its own sake so often relentlessly shamed?

In religious texts, pleasure is often feared as a form of, or path to, gluttony. This is depicted throughout literature. Pleasure is often defined as "pleasure in excess" and blamed for causing imbalance and sin. A person's pleasure is often the cause of harm to them or another. Pleasure-seeking is often seen as something that disconnects a person from devotion to spirit or purity. Shaming people for seeking pleasure, or shaming pleasure altogether, only makes humans recoil on a visceral level. Denying it goes against our natural drive toward sustaining life; it disconnects us from ourselves, from our source. This unmet visceral and spiritual need breeds a void and can lead to all kinds of self-destructive behavior in pursuit of meeting this need. For example, this often occurs in the form of gluttony, a greedy or excessive indulgence. Too much focus on the achievement of one thing is never good. We must parse out our motivations for and our ways of seeking pleasure.

The constant ebb and flow between frustration and soothing involved with the containment of pleasure and bonding creates a cycle of fear and longing. We seek pleasure to sustain ourselves, whether we are aware of it or not, and are constantly trying to work out this internal conflict, both consciously and unconsciously. The conflict and desire to soothe drives us to sustain life.

The need for pleasure cannot be expelled from our being. If we never sought pleasure, we would be lacking in a desire to bond. The wish to live would be in question. Perhaps deflation or depression would occur. When the need for pleasure is coupled with an overwhelming, desperate fear, all libidinal flow might go backward, toward ourselves. This often appears in the form of narcissism. We all have moments of fear, in which we may revert to varying degrees of this kind of behavior. Some have it to the extreme.

These concepts can become a confusing spiral wrapped inside a pretzel, yet they are rampant in society.

Narcissism

We have all heard the word *narcissism*. We've probably all used it or tried to understand someone's behavior by trying to grasp the concept. Ultimately, narcissism is what happens when someone's libidinal flow is not moving out to connect with others. This can be due to some formation through upbringing: emotional overwhelm, rejection, or some other way that their experience of love was conflicted. Because attaching outward has proven terrifying or disappointing, this person feels (unconsciously) isolated and hopeless. Their weak sense of self makes them fear that connecting with others would kill them. No one is going to take care of them. They must take care of themselves in every capacity. The person focuses that energy on themselves as a desperate attempt at self-soothing. The narcissistic tendency—or constant focus on the self in negation of the need for others—does not yield fulfilling pleasure. It is grounded in abstinence from all bonding.

While every motion the narcissist makes toward continued self-soothing is seen by others as a selfish act, the narcissist is truly trying to survive in the only way they have learned is possible. In order to begin to develop an ability to sustain these difficult, frustrating feelings founded in attachments, they need to learn through new experience that it is safe for libidinal flow to move toward others. That empathy will not suffocate or kill them. This person must learn that they won't crumble. This person must do a lot of introspective work. It is a difficult path that varies depending on the level of narcissism—from self-centeredness all the way to psychosis. The most success generally comes from an engagement in some kind of transference-focused therapy with a professional. The same goes for any person who seeks self-soothing and pleasure in destructive ways.

It's confusing, right? We need pleasure, but it can also be our demise.

Self-Destructive Pleasure

You can't give up eating, but you must learn which foods are best for your body and which times you should eat. You must follow that regimen with discipline. If only it were so easy! The painful part about food addiction is learning to understand the parts of your own psyche that seek soothing but fears bonding on such a major level that you are led to obsess and overindulge to the point of self-harm. First, you have to truly want to heal.

In my understanding, the source of painful food relationships is often found in an unconscious wish to separate from or diminish one's true self. This is most often due to fear of experiencing or bonding with one's own being. Perhaps this person has feelings and desires they are ashamed to admit, aggressive thoughts they think make them a bad person, or a deep feeling that they are unlovable. There are many reasons for this lack of identity or existential void. Whatever it is, when the thoughts, feelings, and terrors arise, the person responds with fear-based action. In states of high emotional arousal that are usually defended against, without even realizing they are reacting to anything at all, they run for soothing. The way it plays out in life is unique to each person.

Analysts often consider this fear a result of the person's inability to bond with their mother for some reason unique to their own individual character and relationship. If the infant didn't feel much soothing from the parental bond, their need to feel pleasure developed with a strong retaliation against it. This can begin the process of inflicting harm or pain on themselves in the pursuit of pleasure. You might know someone who has been through overeating, running into relationships that repeatedly cause them emotional pain or physical harm, addictions, alcoholism, cutting or picking skin, or induced vomiting. I'm sure you can think of others.

It's difficult to understand, but it seems that in the moments that the pain is being inflicted, engaging in the act of self-harm gives them great soothing. It may create a feeling of intimacy with the self. In these initial moments, a relief is experienced, deep soothing and calm is felt—until the soothing becomes sickness. The aftereffects, mental and physical depletion, illness, and wounds bring awareness to the reality that they are actually hurting themselves and often others by using self-destruction as a form of soothing. It takes a lot of introspection and proper therapeutic care—an experience of nonobtrusive, unconditional love and organic soothing—to shift a person from a destructive ambivalence toward healthy comfort and pleasure-seeking.

Humans are like chemical equations, oscillating naturally between bonding and individualizing. If these fluid patterns become imbalanced, due to fear of not having enough of one or the other, we become lost in a sea of reactive impulses, seeking to save ourselves from suffocation, submerged to the point of expungement, denied, rejected, or unfed. Gluttony, sloth, pride, rage, lust, greed, and envy—the seven deadly sins—are observed in therapeutic realms not as shameful character flaws but as instinctual impulses toward self-healing, however harmful they may, in fact, be.

Abstinence toward Divine

In Eastern philosophy, there is much discussion of detachment from desire or pleasure-seeking. The external pursuit of pleasure is what causes a rift between spirit and mind. When the mind is not fixated on seeking outside sources of pleasure, the spirit is set free to bond more profoundly with divine energy. This is the ultimate form of soothing. The "monkey mind" in Buddhist psychology obsesses over pleasure and attainment, creating a manic search for a way to quell the longing through material attachment. Many Eastern philosophies say that this is fundamentally due to a fear of the unknown and an inability to feel calm. By letting go of the monkey mind's pursuit of pleasure, going from thing to thing to feel better, they seek soothing through disciplines of abstinence and directed meditation of the mind. Here, the practitioner hopes to find a deeper sense of ease and safety by turning their will over to communing with divine.

Many religions believe in the disconnection from pleasure as a pathway to humility and spiritual attainment. The healing practices in this book are designed to free your body and mind from rigidity and help you open your neural pathways and energy into a consistent flow, expanding circulation.

Sexual Union

We seek sex as a source of pleasure. If you are seeking sex with the goal of quick orgasm in mind, you are most likely looking to fill an emotional need, which often leads to sex addictions. The difference between the goal of orgasm and the quest for sexual union, with a shifted time-space continuum, is that the former is grounded in an active need to find something, attain it, and then move on to search for another—and the latter is a refinement of self-seeking into sensual meditation and tranquility through sexual union to reach higher states of physical health, consciousness, and wisdom.

Humility

Let's not throw the baby out with the bathwater. It is not physical pleasure that is bad. It is the ways that unmet aspects of the self can fall into this bottomless pit of pleasure consumption. I understand that the vibrational light of life can be most effectively found if it is not being desperately sought. Humility is the driving force. We must become very intimate with our longings, our wish to fill an unconscious void. Learn to experience our constant movement from humility to humiliation, understand the space between desire and action, and seek to become attuned to our own repetitive thoughts and seductive urges.

Again, energy never dies; it only transforms. We have a choice over how we perceive and how we act. Needs, wants, thoughts, and feelings are expressions of energy, impulse. They seek to transform libidinal life energy in the body. Let's learn to offer acceptance and validation to the abstract aspects of our mind. Here, we experience less anxiety and become filled by a deeper integration of your true and false self. The insatiable thirst for soothing will not drive us toward self-harm. The chasm between mind and body won't be as great.

Cultivating Organic Pleasure

Pleasure seeking is something we need to do to survive. The pursuit of love and pleasure is woven into all aspects of life, creating myriad effects on mind, body, and relationships throughout each day. Awareness of how we go about the pursuit of fulfillment and pleasure and how we handle it when all of our needs are not met is a pathway to humility and spiritual attainment.

Many people have shut down their ability to enjoy the pleasurable activities we once engaged in naturally as children. We must learn to value and cultivate organic pleasures in adulthood—rather than just finding something like a food, a drug, or a behavior and going after it like an addiction.

Honor your body; it is your temple. A healthy mind-and-body union is your doorway. Let's learn to cultivate organic pleasure from within. This creates a mind-body connection and is a natural form of self-soothing. We free our bodies and minds from rigidity and open our neural pathways and energy. We calm anxiety, and the body circulates more oxygen, blood, and healthy chemicals. Through learning practices to cultivate organic pleasures in the body, we reap the organic benefits that pleasure has on the mind and body.

Organic pleasures are a beautiful celebration of life and love. It is your choice and your freedom to do so. Would you rather be a purveyor of light or a vampire fueled by negativity and latching on to others' energies?

We will learn some practices for cultivating organic pleasure in a few pages. First, let's discuss touch.

Loving Touch

Loving touch gives humans a grounded sense of overall healthy living. Bodily feelings and sensations create emotions that are processed in the brain. Our brains are part of our bodies. It is in your body that you first experience all feelings and sensations. Touch is the most direct connection from one body to another, and loving touch stimulates the pleasure-inducing chemicals that serve to promote the bonding involved in the caretaking required for survival. Loving touch provides this experience more quickly in both the giver's and the receiver's body and brain than any other loving act. Touch is incredibly healing; we are healed through a connection with another living being, especially through touch.

This basic need to connect, to touch, is embedded again in the history of evolution. Let's go back billions of years to the symbiotic

union of single cells, to the first multicellular organisms, to the first life forms on our planet. Throughout time, living things have nurtured this union through the grouping and herding instinct, an instinct that recognizes our essential interconnection with one another and the rest of nature. Particularly in mammals, emotional and physical connection through touching is essential for the survival of offspring. Studies of babies who die for no apparent physical reason in institutions without any loving touch confirm that we cannot survive without the physical caring of being fed and sheltered and without the physical caring of touch.

Why do some people shame the pleasure and touch that heals us? I have read several medical studies centered around the act of touching one person. In the first few moments of receiving touch, a person's natural cell growth accelerates. Within forty-five minutes of being touched, a person's cells and nervous system are calmed, able to recalibrate, which we know allows for more blood circulation, higher endorphin and serotonin levels, and a more balanced state of being. People need to be touched just as much as they need to drink water, eat food, and exercise. We need to touch others and be touched as a healing that helps our cells regenerate, our minds feel lighter, and our bodies become more at ease.

Let us learn to integrate and grow by seeking ways to feel more connected to pleasure. This is why a primary element of healing from trauma and anxiety is centered around giving and receiving healthy, safe touch. Learning to understand what kind of touch feels healing and safe means you are communicating to yourself and the universe that you deserve this kind of experience. Being lovingly held and touched, while focusing on becoming more attuned to the beauty and positive abundance within and around you, are ways you can actively seek healing in your mind and body. Cultivating a radiant healing fuels your body and mind to generate vast quantities of pleasure and love for the survival of self and species.

Let's slow down. The practices I share next are designed to help you cultivate an awareness of what healthy and safe touch feels like and to be able to give yourself organic pleasures when you choose to for the overall health and union of your body and mind.

Mindfulness
Journaling Practice 4

Healing, Safety, and Pleasure

Sit with your journal a bit and ponder your thoughts and feelings on pleasure, love-seeking. Do this exercise at least once a month. Take time to observe your thoughts and feelings every day.

What happens in my body when I long for love? What are the thoughts and words I hear in my mind? When do I find myself most longing for love? Is it before bed? In the morning? Midday lulls? Or does it have nothing to do with time, but rather place, or both? Is it at work? On vacation? Maybe there isn't a specific answer, but does your longing seems to surface depending on the circumstances? After talking to Mom on the phone? Dad? Before taking a meeting that you are fearful of? After? What kinds of wishes occur in your mind during longing? Is it to be held? To be spoken to sweetly? Do you go back to a certain memory or fantasy? When you seek pleasure and soothing, what do you do about it? Do you tell yourself to ignore it? Do you eat, smoke, or drink? When you are craving certain foods, do you stop, observe, and ask yourself what you are truly craving? When and how do you meet your needs in a truly nourishing way? Think about this and begin to observe these moments throughout the day. Really notice how your body feels when you are longing for pleasure, love, and begin to identify this more easily when it comes up. The awareness creates an ability to accept yourself, and when it feels right, take a healthy action toward really giving your mind and body what you are truly craving.

Practice 4: Journaling on Touch

Sit with your journal a bit and ponder your thoughts and feelings about pleasure and touch. Return to journaling these questions once a month. Observe yourself daily!

Please note that these questions are also very helpful for people who have been through sexual trauma. Many people who have experienced unsafe touch against their will hold a numbness in their body and an anxiety around being touched. These issues are delicate and take many years to heal. Some people never fully recover but find ways to become more conscious of the ways the trauma has affected them, and they are able to decipher between posttraumatic stress reactions and recovery responses. Let's be patient with ourselves and begin to explore how we respond and relate to touch as a means to heal and recover.

❀ Do you find yourself repeatedly returning to touch or tactile means to try to get a feeling of aliveness? Do you experience nourishing depth of quality? Or do you find yourself needing to repeat, repeat, repeat rather than adjust your ability to give and receive?

❀ Do you find yourself generally using vision to gather information for your mind? Or are you also able to use your sense of sight to take in sensory feelings or even texture? What else comes to mind for you as an individual when you write about touch as a form of enlivening?

❀ In what ways do you experience shame or negative thoughts around giving or receiving touch?

❀ How can you use touch (on yourself or with others) throughout the day to stimulate your energy in subtle ways?

Think about how you use your senses and which ones create the deepest and richest experiences for you throughout the day. Think about what quality over quantity means in terms of your sensory experiences. Return to the senses and sensations that are the most soothing as a way to explore and deepen your positive relationship to touch and sensation.

Practice 4: Cultivating Healthy Pleasure

Hear my voice as we shift into a short meditation on healthy pleasure.

Begin to see yourself now and always as an organic being that is gifted with the power and ability to consciously create more pleasure, more love in your being and in the world.

Slow down and go through the first three practices I have taken you through so far. By now, they should be an easy flow, intertwined as you open your breath. Attune, sense within and around you, and accept whatever you are feeling now. There is no right or wrong way to feel. Sit within whatever you are feeling now.

Start to become aware of your body. Many people are actually numb. Are you numb right now? Is your mind stirring but your body feeling very little? Yikes! You deserve to fully feel, sense, touch, and smell. Gaze. I am going to ask you to do three simple things right now.

First, put your fingertips together. Feel the sweet, sensitive pads on the tops of your fingertips. Breathe in and rub your fingertips together for about a minute. Concentrate on the center of your tips. You might feel a tingling, a pressure, or some sensation. If you do, see if you can shape and play with this source, moving your fingers farther apart and then closer together. You will notice that you can feel this energy force between your fingers, and you can mold and shape it.

Pick up a rose or a succulent flower. Touch the inside petals, feel the moisture, and run your fingertips along the skin of the flower. Smell it. Inhale the sweet essential scent that the flower offers you. Allow yourself to become consumed with running your tongue along the flower petals. Taste the flower. Run your fingers and the flower along your ear. Hear the beautiful smooth sound of a soft touch upon your ear. Let your eyes consume the flower's pores, as though your eyes are fingertips. Feel the flower's touch through your body. Breathe.

You can do these simple pleasure-enhancing exercises anytime throughout the day. When you eat, really taste and smell the flavors of the food. Slow down. When you see, allow the sight to touch your inner being. Feel your clothes upon your skin. Become attuned to all that you see, touch, hear, smell, and taste throughout each day. These simple acts nourish your pleasure receptors, melt the numbness, calm your mind, and open you up to the true essence. You are an organic being. This is your calling and your healing.

I am talking about the senses in your body because you can touch your body internally through your senses all day long—even when you are not touching another person. This will open you up to wanting to truly touch another with the intention of giving and receiving love. Not in a needy way that you need the person to open your senses for you, but in a way that you are already an orbiting, open, flowing, expansive being in your own body. When you touch another, you are truly touching with the healing properties of connecting to a higher life force through union with one another.

Mindful Meditation

Practice 4

Cultivating Healthy Pleasure through Safe Touch

Here is a simple step-by-step exercise that can be practiced at any time. Open your body and breathe as a tune-up before beginning your day—so it stays with you in your mindful daily observance.

- ✲ Lay flat on your back. Feel the foundation beneath you supporting your body, touch your body sensually on any part of your skin.
- ✲ Rub your fingertips together.
- ✲ Breathe into your diaphragm muscle. Don't stop on the inhale or exhale. Let it be steady in any sensations you feel internally, in and out with no holding. If you find yourself holding or stopping breath at all during this exercise, it usually means your chatter mind is activated. This is fine. Gently bring your breath back to your body, and finding sensation to connect with, expand through breath.
- ✲ Trace your fingers along your skin. We are warming up your senses, your body. I would like you to begin with erogenous zones that you enjoy (please do not

go to your genitals since we are learning to enliven your entire somatic organ: your skin) touch the insides of your forearm, your neck, your lips, your abdomen. Try fast, sweeping touch; try kneading, try palm, try fingers; try light, feather touch. Find what areas you like and don't like. Long, slow strokes. Touch yourself exactly as you like to be touched, slowly. Very slowly. Feel each pore, each tremble, each warm pocket.

☼ Stroke your skin, your soma. Breathe.

☼ Feel the steady expansion and release of breath. Tune in to any sensations you feel inside your body. Sometimes we feel most around our abdomen, liver, kidneys, or heart. These are all creating internal stimuli because they are hard at work cleansing and circulating energy and blood through your body, so there is already more sensation in these areas.

☼ Allow your breath to go into your pelvis. Let your fingers slowly trace the space between your pelvic bones.

☼ Breathe all the way down to your root chakra, lower spine, and back.

☼ Touch your heart, breathe.

☼ Allow your body to surrender to gravity and drop more deeply down into the foundation on which you lay.

☼ Continue to breathe into all of your expanding body sensations, sending breath

> A deep, abiding integrated connection with out generative sensuality is the necessary foundation of our authentic expression and participation in the world. This provides a constant stream of encounters with our essential soulful self; We support the unfolding healing of human bodies, cultures and earth.
> —Cassie Moore, Caffyn Jesse, and Mehdi Darvish Yahya, *Healers on the Edge*

between your root. As you exhale, feel the heat, the sensation, and the energy moving toward your heart.

 Breathe all the way out as you exhale and drop down even more deeply into your pelvis as you inhale.

Practice this for a while. Feel your mind and body synchronize in the safe and healthy environment you have created for yourself.

Mantra

I am creating a safe space for myself to experience my given energy, love, and healing touch. This is nourishing for my soul. I deserve to feel safe and loved. I will give this to myself and ask the universe to hold me safe and healthy.

Chapter 5

Emotion

In this chapter, we will discuss emotions. I will explain how the physiology of emotion and conscious emotion are related to trauma and PTSD. These concepts are core elements for understanding the role emotions play in your healing and self-awareness. At the close of this chapter, journaling and meditation practices will lead you through practical questions and techniques to help you understand the practical use of a concept called *interoception* for somatic body awareness and develop a positive technique for checking in with your emotional state throughout the day.

What is a feeling? Where do emotions come from? What do they mean? Are the varying emotions we all experience the same for each person—or are they individualized sensations and ideas based on our own bodies and brains? What do emotional responses teach us about ourselves? We each uniquely process the stimuli that enter, and are created, in our bodies. It is in your brain that stimuli become emotions.

The Brain and Nervous System

An isolated single-celled organism responds to significant events, external or internal stimuli, through shifts in its vibrational pulse, such as changing in shape and temperature. External stimuli come from outside circumstances, like loud sounds, changes in light, touch, pressure, heat, and cold. Internal stimuli are generated from within the organism's cellular vibration and often are reacting to external, which create reverberations of new responses from the initial input.

For example, if you change the outside light source, a plant will shift direction and begin to move toward that new light source, and then new growth will sprout. The plant's internal, cellular wisdom toward promoting survival creates this shift without the need for conscious thought or cognition. This is the mysterious, spontaneous force of nature pulsing throughout and interconnecting all. Learning to perceive this life flow within all of us as sacred, practicing the cultivation and raising of libidinal flow in our bodies and minds, is the union of body, mind, and spirit.

Plasticity of Brain

Adaptive shifts occur naturally when outside circumstances change; a new approach toward securing survival becomes necessary for sustenance. Decay, shedding, and fresh libidinal, cellular growth occurs all the time. This same theme manifests through human emotions. The body and brain take in, process, and naturally adapt, creating new cognition or awareness.

Humans have a great ability to adapt; we are able to consciously go beyond limitations beholden to primitive survival responses. The mind and body can identify emotional decay: emotions and responses that are no longer helpful to our sustenance. We can process, recycle, expel toxic behavior, and develop new perceptions, new life choices. This doesn't happen quickly. It is achieved through consistent observance and containment of active response. Humans have the ability to hold back, reflect, analyze their choice of behavior, make adjustments, and form new responses to the same stimuli. Humans can also become conscious of new engagements and new environments and adapt to fresh stimuli.

This ability to make new choices and responses is due to the evolution of the brain and the adaptability of synaptic pathways. Neural pathways shift when internal awareness, behavior, responses, and stimuli input change. The brain has the ability to create new memories and new ways of being. Old patterns or choices can seem to become part of a distant past—if remembered at all. This is a very powerful aspect of our emotional and chemical comprehension of our experience in the world.

Physiology of Emotion and Conscious Emotion

Physiology of emotion is the state of feeling closely linked to the nervous system, which results in physical and psychological changes due to varying states and strengths of arousal. Emotional physiology occurs at a primitive level, and behavior manifests before the emotion is perceived or named. We see this often in PTSD or trauma-related reactions to internal and external stimuli.

Emotions have their origin in sensation that begins in the body and are then processed by the brain: memory, fantasy, thought, and consciousness. Emotional pain has the same type of reflexive response as physiological—the experience of the stimulus leads to the arousal—but then we have emotion. Humans feel both arousal and emotion in response to noxious stimuli. The sound of a gunshot leads to physiological responses like rapid heart rate and trembling—and the subjective experience of fear.

Conscious emotion results from the brain, heart, and body acting in concert. If you think about pain, suffering, or any emotional response, it is a private experience that is altogether dependent upon the perception of that unique organism. This creates you.

Why don't we always choose what is best for us?

Emotions and Survival

Emotions are often inspired by a behavioral tendency relating to a particular motivation. Fear makes us retreat from perceived dangers. Protective emotion makes us risk survival by facing a threat rather than running away. Pleasure and happiness make us rest, eat, and find joy. Emotions compound the pleasure and comfort of being near those we trust. They keep us banded together for greater protection, and emotions are complex. Human emotions don't always work to our perceived advantage.

We aren't growing up in a simple predator/prey environment. We learn to communicate to caregivers when we're in distress. The origin of the feelings/emotions comes from the changing chemical balance due to levels of stimulation and frustration within us. Our natural temperament and the culture around us—society, geography, politics, and religion—form our perceptions of the world, and we learn what emotions are and how to name them. Everything we consume, the environment (including toxins), and age-directed physiological maturation and related changes within our bodies cause us to feel different things. Some dramatic changes, even apparent shifts in perception, character, and response, can signal adverse changes in our emotional state, including medical conditions.

An environment, especially a bad childhood environment, can trigger our emotions. Emotions can cause anxiety, and the experience of stimuli in the body or mind can create intrapsychic images and mental feelings that are overwhelming. Sometimes, changes are purely simulated in the brain maps. This is observable in humans and animals as "mirror neurons." When we feel sympathy for a sick person, we recreate that person's pain to a certain degree internally.

Maladaptive Defense

We can sometimes adopt a mode of survival that doesn't appear to be necessarily healthy, but we do it anyway. Someone who grew up in an abusive environment may still see dangers as an adult where there are none. Someone who grew up without dependable love may seek closeness that isn't safe. Someone who grew up without support may perceive everyone as selfish and feel wary of closeness. If you look at these responses closely, this person is still seeking survival.

Our minds and bodies are always intuitively seeking soothing, pleasure, comfort, and protection. Often what is familiar (conditioned responses) gives us this feeling and will give our nervous system a feeling of calm, even in discomfort, but what is familiar is not always best for our health. This is a maladaptive response. The motivation is libidinal in that it is spawned from a wish to survive, but the outcome can be the opposite. We know the general outcome of the action; it is uncomfortable, but we know where it leads. Intuitively, we know how much our psyche can handle, and that change from familiar to unfamiliar (known to unknown) will cause greater stress in the foreground. This is a repetitive cycle of hope and disappointment; this survival mode leaves us feeling powerless over change—but still able to survive.

Humans do have the ability to change the neural pathways of learned emotional response. Through repeated frustrations combined with therapeutic introspection, the human mind can learn new ways of perceiving and acting. The ability to handle unfamiliar stimuli can be strengthened over time. The human mind and body can become conditioned with new memory, developing new meaning and new affect, when a person develops the ability to accept and sustain frustration and other difficult feelings.

Often, engaging in modalities such as talk therapy, bodywork, breath, meditation, exercise, and energy balancing can help a person learn to sit through, identify, and express uncomfortable feelings without going into action. A child learns to talk, ask for what it needs, or attain it on their own or not. An adult mind must continuously engage in verbalizing feelings and desires without taking action to fix the feeling right away. Through this process, the feelings become less powerful. A hierarchical level of body stimulation and brain perception happens, creating deeper mind-and-body union and awareness. Let us continue to evolve with greater breadth of emotional experience, deeper levels of intimacy with self and others, growth and expansion of life experiences and successes. A beautiful hug of life force.

What role do emotions play? What role does your body play? We have talked about our relationship to ourselves and the world outside, and their roots in infant primary-care relations. Learning to sustain the frustration of not getting what we instinctually crave creates individual ways of expressing and seeking different kinds of character and personality. The superego (how we want to be seen and received socially) is developed through how we relate to authority and what others think of us.

As we grow beyond primary care, we redirect our libidinal needs toward others. This forges a deeper relationship with the full range of our desire and emotional needs. As all energy seeks to be transformed, these memories and feelings want to be expressed and understood. Many get discharged through fantasy, dreams, and body language. Some people express emotion by pointing to parts of their body and saying, "It's blocked here," "I'm sobbing in my heart," or "I cannot feel myself." Some of these feelings or primitive memories are expressed in mindless action, psychosomatic issues, or speech, dermatological, or physical ailments. We can develop awareness by learning to embody emotion and slowly integrating it into the conscious self.

Consciousness, Emotion, and Desire

Consciousness, much like feelings, is based on a representation of the body and mind. We can possess feelings only when the mind can create a representation of the body's reactions to certain stimuli and the related changes that occur in the brain. In this way, we can perceive them. Our image of ourselves is the only one we know how to adapt in an ever-changing environment. Emotions alone—without conscious feelings—would not be enough. Without self-image, there would be no consciousness. The brain constantly needs up-to-date information on the body's state to regulate all the processes that keep us alive.

Subjective consciousness is the ability to observe your own consciousness. Subjective is a word we use when attempting to parse out our emotional response to what is going on around us. Sometimes our response is formed solely based on our experience. It is helpful if we can learn to develop objective consciousness since it increases awareness, empathy, and intimacies with self and others.

Emotions have their origin in the universal human state of wanting something. If you subjectively observe your mind, you will become convinced that wanting is the primary source of your emotions. In fact, all that occurs in the world starts with desire or wanting. You are what your deepest desire is—as your desire is your intention. Your intention is your will—as your will is your deed. Your deed is your destiny.

Intent is a seed of consciousness. If you pay attention, intent has within it the means for its own fulfillment. The ability is lost when your self-image overshadows your self and when you sacrifice your true self for how you want others to see you. You can restore the power of intent through self-awareness. It reestablishes connection to unity when you have awareness of your desires in proportionate relationship to those of others and to your universal interconnection to all living things. Through developing awareness of your mind and body, you can begin to let go of fear-based desire to manipulate, control, or criticize. You can become able to feel, see, and hear your true desires and discover a path to nurturing, empathetic relationships.

It's easier said than done, but it's never impossible to progress!

Feel Your Feelings!

Physiological emotion (feelings) are core sensations within the body that tell you something needs to be addressed or healed within. These feelings may be physical heartache because you have been deeply hurt by an expression of rejection from yourself or from someone else or the feeling of a rapid heartbeat because you are in fear of experiencing the feeling or being rejected. You might be experiencing a tight, restricted throat because you are unable to speak your truth. These examples are feelings or core sensations in your body and are not fully processed by your mind.

You can literally feel your feelings. Often, expressions of your unconscious are difficult. Your mind may begin to tell a story about the origin of the feelings. This is a way that your mind begins to perceive, respond, and understand. You might not be able to put the feelings into words. It is better to feel first. Trust that your feeling is communicating something and try to allow yourself to follow the response (crying, anger, or joy). It is a grace in action when you allow your feelings to be put into motion. This is a healthy way to begin to release stored feelings. When your unconscious is given time and permission to release the stored pain, it will provide space and relieve the pressure of the stored-up energy. Your mind and body can begin to communicate more fluidly. You can begin to understand.

Your mind needs something to do. Give it something to do by attuning to your body sensations or listening within. Engaging your mind in this way can become a daily practice in your life as a movement toward self-understanding and healing. Your quality of life will change because this practice begins to allow you to open and move past the deadness or defensive layers that we are often naturally surrounded by due to socialization and the stereotypical ways we are taught to relate to ourselves and others. Dropping below the mental-emotional accumulations instinctually builds a bridge between the false self (a socially constructed sense of self) and the true self that resides deep within. Focusing your mind on attuning to your feelings can help you move past rational verbal layers of conversation in your mind and in your social life. You can come to terms with your truth and falsehood. This is the path to understanding how circumstances affect your internal self. You can continue to learn about yourself by tuning into your body to feel your emotions and then listening and watching your mind. This brings about balance between the body, mind, and heart.

At some point, some of your emotions may serve as a defense against experiencing deeper emotions. For example, rage often masks sadness. Try listening to your feelings more thoughtfully. When you are fluidly open to this, you will develop even deeper awareness and mind-body union. We do the best we can; when we are ready to feel the deep grieving, we will. We don't have to feel the hardest feelings alone; we can ask for help and work through these layers in therapy. We also need to laugh and have fun!

Interoception

Interoception is the ability to monitor the physiological condition of your body. This forges an intimate connection between the physical sensations of your body and the emotions that arise in response. Most of us are aware of our heartbeat, bladder pressure, and hunger to some degree. We all have wide variability in how sensitive we are—sometimes more than others.

Your emotional range and capabilities are linked to how well you are able to perceive the physical sensations within your heart and other parts of your body. People who have a capacity to feel the internal state of their own body have been shown to be more intuitive, experience stronger emotional arousal, have better memory for emotional material, and are better able to control their negative emotions. This connection between the physical sensations in your body and your emotions extends to the neural processes in our brain. Developing an awareness of your bodily feelings is important for developing awareness of your emotional response. People who display an imbalance or defense against interoceptive awareness are less able to have positive emotions in daily life, have more difficulty with decisions, and so on. Training the mind to be more internally aware will lead to heightened emotional abilities and health.

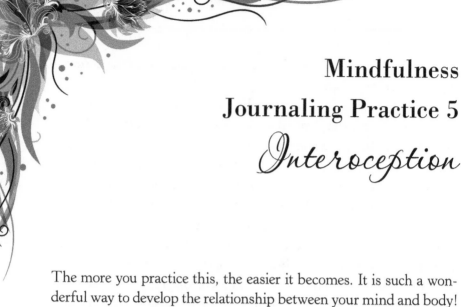

Mindfulness
Journaling Practice 5
Interoception

The more you practice this, the easier it becomes. It is such a wonderful way to develop the relationship between your mind and body!

I invite you to begin exploring mind-and-body awareness by journaling. The best way to find out what is happening between your mind and body is to look and listen within. These questions may seem complex. Give yourself time and patience with them. Write every few weeks. We are attuning ourselves to a new way of perceiving. It takes time and repetition. Writing can open doors in your mind that may otherwise remain closed. The repetition of positive mind-and-body practices is essential to unlearn negative behaviors, thoughts, and emotions:

1. Sit. Observe. Breathe. Feel. What do I feel in my own body? In my heart? Where do I feel the most sensation in my body? What does it feel like? Temperature, heart rate, organ pulse, numbness, pain? If it had words, what would it say? Do I have certain ailments that are recurring? Where are they? Pain, stinging, throbbing? If it had words, what would it say? Do I want to be with this feeling—or do I want to move away?

2. Move your attention to the inside of your brain. Navigate its many parts, layers, and sections. Try to put your awareness in the middle of your

brain. Imagine what it looks like. What are the thoughts generating from this part of my brain? Emotions? What is my brain telling me? Telling my body? Move to the front of your brain, behind your forehead. See it. What are the thoughts here? Are they faster than the ones in the center? What are they saying? Do I see images? Are there emotions? What does this part of my brain say or feel about my body? Move your awareness to the back of your brain, the top of your spinal cord. Try to see it. What is generating from this part of my brain? What are the feelings or sensations here? Do I see images? What is it saying? Does it want to say something to my body? Are there emotions? Imagine an energy moving fluidly between the circuits of your brain. Imagine that it is weaving the parts of your brain together. What do you feel? See? Hear? Is there someone's voice in your brain saying anything to you? About you? Do you hear fears? Longings?

3. Ask yourself. How can I tell whether I am experiencing a feeling in my body or emotion in my brain that needs or wants to be expressed or released? How can I identify when I am creating the emotion from my own thought? What feelings arise most for me now? Do I cry (insert any emotion you do identify)? Where do I feel this in my body? What does it feel like? Are you feeling this for a reason? Do I feel it often? Or is it unfounded? Notice how your mind responds when your body has a feeling. Do I immediately begin thinking? Can I focus my mind on the feeling? Does energy need to be released? Can I let myself? Does this feel like a defense against an even deeper feeling? How do I know? Can I be patient with my own process?

4. Think about something that is bothering you about another person. What am I feeling? What do I want to say? What do I want to have happen? Think about the situation objectively, imagining you are the other person.

How do I think they feel? How have they expressed this to me? What have they expressed? Is my perception of how they feel solely based on my own experience? Am I able to be objective? Does my empathy for the other aspects involved inform my perception and emotional response?

Meditation Practice 5

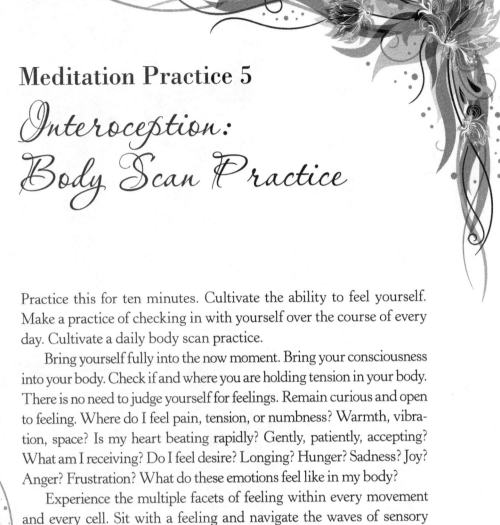

Interoception: Body Scan Practice

Practice this for ten minutes. Cultivate the ability to feel yourself. Make a practice of checking in with yourself over the course of every day. Cultivate a daily body scan practice.

Bring yourself fully into the now moment. Bring your consciousness into your body. Check if and where you are holding tension in your body. There is no need to judge yourself for feelings. Remain curious and open to feeling. Where do I feel pain, tension, or numbness? Warmth, vibration, space? Is my heart beating rapidly? Gently, patiently, accepting? What am I receiving? Do I feel desire? Longing? Hunger? Sadness? Joy? Anger? Frustration? What do these emotions feel like in my body?

Experience the multiple facets of feeling within every movement and every cell. Sit with a feeling and navigate the waves of sensory awareness happening in your body. Is anger pulsating waves of tension? Is deep sadness or even some kind of strange pleasure residing within the anger? The further you can drop into the anger, the more you will begin to notice that it will shift, change, move, and find expression. This is a primitive state of self-exploration. You are exploring stimuli. Let the feeling emote. If your mind wants to jump in or your body wants to clamp down, put your attention back on the feeling. As you move into it and through it, feel. Remember that you are bringing up feelings from within your body and your cells. They need to be released from your being.

Chapter 6

Anxiety, Addiction, and Obsession

Cultivate your ability to open your heart. Look into the eyes of another, gaze in stillness together, and be with the subtle shifts that naturally occur inside of you and them together. Do not try to figure it out or decide—just be within stillness together. Breathe.

In this chapter, I will define the concepts of anxiety, addiction, and obsession. I will explain how trauma may affect your ability to be with yourself and why people seek unhealthy, outside attachments to feel better. Healthy love and pleasure-seeking can help relieve the negative effects of trauma. I will explain how learning to find healthy ways to fill your mind  and body with a sense of true confidence and love are elements for the foundational healing of trauma, awakening the body-and-mind connection. At the close of this chapter, journaling and meditation practices will lead you through practical questions and techniques to help you understand negative self-talk and the gap between true self and false self.

What Is Anxiety?

Anxiety has many different connotations. Anxiety can be defined so broadly. I would like to discuss the ways in which anxiety feels in your body, how your mind often chooses to relate to it, and what we can do to begin to calm ourselves from within. Feel welcome to write anything down while reading this passage. Getting ideas out of the mind helps bring a feeling of relief, and seeing it written down gives us an opportunity to observe objectively what we are experiencing viscerally. Anxiety is a bodily sensation, an emotion, and an idea. Anxiety usually feels like unease, worry, and nervousness.

How does anxiety feel in your body? How does your mind often choose to relate to it? How can you calm this dis-ease, beyond a quick fix (unsustainable solution) like numbing yourself? Knowing the hows and whys may help you. Let's look within at the internal conflict.

Many people have written or spoken to me about not getting quality sleep or not having energy. Many express frustration and restlessness. Many feel dissatisfied. At the root is a deep, persistent anxiety. Many people never learned to address and understand themselves emotionally, and they picked up all kinds of anxieties and chaotic, emotional repetitions.

If you are like most people, you may worry at times about paying bills, getting to work on time, or what outfit you are going to wear today. There is no delineating a more substantial anxiety from a lesser one. All anxiety is a communication that some conflict is occurring. The anxiety is not from the conflict. It springs from the wish to be rid of or fix the conflict. Anxiety is an aspect of yourself that beckons for you to listen and understand. It is an invitation to know yourself more deeply. Anxiety can be sneaky, and it arrives in many forms. Let's get to know anxiety.

Free-Floating Anxiety

Free-floating anxiety is a general feeling that something is just not right. You might know what I'm talking about. You wake up or be walking down the street, and although nothing bad has happened, your body feels tense—and your mind is jabbering on that something is off in your world. Most often, this anxiety surfaces in thoughts. Your mind is telling you you're not good enough or you're too fat/skinny, too greedy, not powerful enough at work, or not loved enough. Usually it resides as an undercurrent of feeling that colors your day.

This free-floating anxiety—actually all forms of anxiety—often arises when you have begun negating your internal world, suppressing feelings, or getting stuck in a negative perception of yourself through comparison.

Negative Self-Talk

Emotions are energy in motion. It is damaging to our well-being when we suppress feelings. When we suppress feelings, we experience anxiety. This anxiety often takes the form of negative mind chatter and psychosomatic responses. Negative mind chatter and repetitive thoughts might be unfelt or deep sensitivities of the inner child.

Often, repetitive thoughts are based on illusion—distorted beliefs, a feeling that you are a victim, blaming others, or judging yourself and others. This mind chatter is our maladaptive attempt at survival, trying to protect us from pain. Mind chatter employs this defense by keeping us in the world of illusions, keeping our attention on negative beliefs from our painful past and protecting us from encountering any pain in the future. Unfortunately, it backfires, and our attention to our repetitive negative thoughts attracts more negative experiences to us, which becomes a self-fulfilling prophecy. The mind chatter will keep us from clarity, hearing our wisdom, and devoting our energies to cultivating awareness and our highest good.

Repetitive mind chatter is like a siren going off, beckoning us to pay attention to what is really going on within. Our feelings are ours to explore, and if we fear them, we get stuck. We are energy. We are not our minds. We can always depend on one truth: if we sit with a feeling or let it live inside of us, allowing the feeling freedom and expression, it will transform. This simple act calms our inner tension, much like it often calms the anxieties of a screaming infant. The negativity loses power as a calming fluidity sets in. We will begin to naturally let go of any negative energies within our being. This transformation will direct us toward clarity of thought, emotional perspective, and conscious action.

If we do not allow ourselves time and space to feel our feelings, the negative mind chatter will increase, and emotions will build and be stored in our energy fields, which will lead to emotional outbursts, continued problems, and sometimes disease in the body.

Existential Anxiety

The enigmatic force twisted inside almost all of our anxieties roots back to a fear of the unknown. Existentially, we are always grappling with these questions. Why and how do I exist on this planet? You might not consciously ask, but you may take actions to override the feeling in pursuit of proving worthiness or strength.

A primitive human instinct, from the core of our reptilian brain is to compare and compete. This instinct may help us survive if we are only consumed by competition. This has an unfortunate side effect on our internal nature and overall survival.

Much of society is based on trying to answer fears with material power and willpower. We are often socially conditioned to check our worthiness for being alive by judging ourselves and others by what life looks like on the outside and striving to take and have more.

Let's separate the beast from the human. Let's strive to evolve beyond killing others to take what we think we need or deserve. Let's find strength and empowerment through bonding. First, we have to bond with ourselves.

Motivation

Natural drive is a force of libidinal energy. If we don't have drive, we are depressed. Ambition is important. Everyone has the desire to create in life. It is the life force's instinct toward survival and fulfillment. If we often feel anxious, dissatisfied, or disoriented, it is important to look at what motivates our drive.

Persona

When it comes to feeling deeply satisfied, the external person you can create and show to others is always going to feel insufficient on some level. This is because persona or the false self is built on comparison to others. Many people feel internally bankrupt and learn to quickly gain their sense of social identity through grouping rather than bonding.

Grouping is when you become affiliated with external circumstances because you want others to see you a certain way. It is a proverbial flag to wave. Fitting in seems easily accomplished for the most part by attending a certain school, being a part of a certain company or institution, winning awards, appearing to be in a successful relationship, wearing trendy brands, having your children in certain schools, driving a certain car, feeling empowered by money, career, and beauty, or even rooting for a certain team.

Is any of this wrong? It's not wrong to be or want to be accomplished, want nice things, have prestigious professional or academic credentials, look great, or be part of a group because you are all rooting for a certain team! This is all wonderful for morale, drive, and a place to channel your energy!

However, this kind of externalized grouping is often motivated by a bankrupt internal self. External solutions are sought as a quick fix for lack of true confidence and from a wish to fit in. This can be motivated by a feeling that this is the only way others will validate you. Validating others and being validated by others based on these external circumstances is for the most part dissatisfying.

We all go to sleep at night, wake up, and ask, "What am I really meant to do? Who am I really meant to be? Why am I here? What is the point? What do I care about? What do I believe in?" These dark nights of the soul are moments when the spirit is seeking confidence from deep within. Somewhere inside, we know these externals can dissolve, turn on us, or be washed away at any moment. When these material variables waver, as they always do, we are left feeling dissatisfied and anxious. We have built nothing sustainable to fall back on, to fill ourselves with.

Drive motivated by a need to prove our existence, assuage the fear of the unknown, and find well-being through selling persona often puts our minds in the future. We become consumed by anxieties, thinking about how to be more successful, planning strategies for developing more, and making bigger social strides. When this powerful drive isn't grounded in presence and is only in the mind, ego, and aggressive use of the body energies, then ambition, competitive drive, and goals can become our most destructive opponents. Anxiety takes over. Anxiety blocks our ability to manifest successfully and healthfully. Even if something wonderful is happening, we are anxious to get to the next thing. If we lose social persona, what are we?

You do not cultivate vibrancy and strength through willpower and material wealth. Let's get interested in internal development over short-term topical solutions. I am all for being successful, wealthy, and deeply rooted to true self-confidence, heart, and empathy. We were not put on this earth to learn that suffering poverty gives us a greater heart. Actually, losing everything really does help a person gain deep confidence and humility. You rebuild because you have goals. Your goals are sprung from a natural instinct for abundance. We all gain satisfaction through accomplishing a goal. We often learn the most about ourselves by seeing this goal through, not giving up, and believing in our visions.

When we get all our confidence in our livelihood from people, places, and things—if you're only conscious of the external world—that winning high quickly fades. A repetitive pattern of becoming dependent on how others perceive you takes over, and you have to go out and get a new win. We can become ungrounded by the ability to let go of results, anxiously caught in a circle of dissatisfactions and disillusions, and caught up in the familiar place of thinking, *This isn't right either.* The cycle becomes emotionally/energetically draining—and we lose. Constantly seeking external satisfaction almost sounds like drug addiction.

Often, people do turn to quick fix, feel-good remedies to alleviate any internal self-questioning or anxiety. We are often trained by medical professionals, respected elders, elected appointees, and advertisers to take a drink or a pill or binge on TV to feel better. Comfort food and quick sex also serve as powerful ways to escape, relieve, soothe, comfort our internal unease and conflict—for the moment.

Again, there are two sides to every coin. Self-soothing is a quest for survival. It is a human instinct to want to feel better, and it is a sign of a wish to live. Entertainment, food, and other soothing devices can stimulate pleasure receptors in the body and mind, which is not a bad thing. The problem is that often when we hit the substances and externals as ways to enhance pleasure and avoid knowing ourselves, we actually deplete the natural wellsprings of pleasure in our bodies. We fall short quickly, feeling much lower than we did before we sought the soothing. Anxiety returns, and we have to run back to that thing. It is a conundrum in its own right.

Addiction

Addictions can be born out of a series of moments when we sense a void. In discomfort or anxiety, we can quickly reach for something to fill or numb it. It could be food, nicotine, alcohol, sex, anger, energy drinks, pain pills, or the internet. Let's look at what may be going on with us.

If we live life disconnected from our senses, live in our heads, our minds, struggling to fight against, or bypass experience through logic, we often feel tired, angry, lonely—and we don't know why.

Unfortunately, as a society, we are fed a prescription for anxiety that is centered around drug reliance: pharmaceuticals or substances that quickly calm the nervous system. Many learn early in life to use substances for numbing, as a way to "chill out" or "push into oblivion," giving us a way to deny unwanted feelings. It makes sense. If we have not learned to understand, deal with these large vats of stimulation entering our bodies, don't want to live in our bodies, listen to our mind chatter, we have to find ways to deal with them.

Learning to become aware of the mind and body as a foundation for maturation is not the general focus of our society. Instead, society uses character modification through moral prohibitions and shaming aspects of the self as a means for maintaining order. Then it punishes bad behavior when the unaccepted, unprocessed feelings come out sideways. So many people, the punishing authorities included, don't know how to be with their inner life or see the world as a whole.

For many people, being alone brings a sense of dread. Is it boredom? Loneliness? Being confronted with your own thoughts and feelings? Many people who dread being alone are uncomfortable feeling themselves. This struggle can be linked to deeper issues within the psyche and soma and is often especially true for people who have been through trauma or experienced anxiety. Loneliness is connected to loss, grief, lack of self-esteem, trauma, and insecurity. Becoming introspective and more aware of what you experience in your inner life will help guide you to a stronger self-confidence and love. Having a strong circle of community and a strong ability to attune to yourself cultivated through self-care is important. Being alone is a part of human existence. Loneliness is also part of the human condition. Let's learn to be with the unknown, the loneliness, and begin to enjoy solitude and the exploration of our inner lives. The other side of that coin is chronic pathological overwhelm, a condition that can lead to depression, anxiety, obsession, and addiction. Let's explore.

Maturation into adulthood is generally taught as a separation from self and body, to follow rules and fit in. People are also taught to mask and internalize feelings rather than finding healthy ways to process and express them. It's not surprising that so many people find, as they mature, that they need to put substances in their body and mind to be able deal with fear, powerlessness, and overstimulation. As a culture, we are offered substances as a shortcut to body, mind, and spiritual union. Natural tools like nature, breathing, exercise, and disciplining the mind are rarely discussed as ways to calm the nervous system and express emotion.

However, many people learn to use substances as a way to "enter the present moment." Many calm the nervous system, raise endorphins, serotonin, and oxytocin, and bring a person into a moment of serenity. Other drugs raise adrenaline and sharpen beta-alanine for clear focus of the mind and increased confidence. These substances often deplete the neuroreceptors and transmitters that create and receive natural, organic chemicals. When we aren't on the substance, we feel even more depleted. This leads to addictions or dependence. Perhaps society has the right idea, but addiction and dependence are rampant in society and cause health, family, and economic problems for many people.

Taking in the present moment—through your senses, meditation, exercise, talk, nature, and bonding—enhances the natural creation of these organic body and brain chemicals: serotonin, endorphin, oxytocin, beta-alanine, and others. Natural chemicals promote and sustain cellular growth by calming the nervous system and promoting the development of healthy, balanced chemistry and cells rather than mutated ones. Mutated cells are the foundation for cancer growths and other illnesses.

The gamut of emotional disorders is vast. I respect the short-comings of mental health care and the painful issues that drive us to it. The issues are real. Some people need medication for debilitating mental illness. Still, serious mental problems are often overmedicated by professionals, resulting in painful side effects, including long-term liver problems, neurological impairments, and dependency. It remains true, however, that medication, supplemented by talk therapy and a healthier living regime may yield sustainable results. Postop care often requires medication, though we have seen an overwhelming epidemic of addiction to painkillers in the US, which for many, began with repeated surgeries and irresponsible postop care.

I am addressing the use of pharmaceutical, street drugs, and addictive substances to get a quick sense of calmness and escape emotions and anxieties. Even in these instances, they are highly individualized.

Many people have been through massive trauma in life and are doing the best they can to survive. They seek the soothing of drugs and alcohol, even for those who haven't necessarily been through trauma but have high anxieties due to upbringing, social conditioning, or bullying. Addiction is a serious, fatal issue.

Addiction is often considered a low-level attempt or reprieve of sorts, a need to feel connected to something calming. Substances can instantly quell anxiety and rid a person of unwanted memories or fears about the future. While this is helpful in the moment, it does not train your body to create natural calm and balance through perspective, spiritual understanding, trust, and awareness practices that promote natural well-being.

There are many detrimental outcomes for taking this shortcut to acceptance through substances: cellular imbalance, disease, mental and physical imbalance, increased anxiety, fear of the past and future increases. Often people make serious life decisions while under the influence of substances, thinking they are calmer and more aware. They fall into endless repetition, unhealthy communication styles, avoidance, passivity, aggression, rage, repression, physical fatigue, lack of courage, and so on.

I am interested in internal development over short-term, topical solutions. Quick-fix choices to assuage anxiety and emotion under these influences cause a person to travel down a deviated path, off of intuitive, synchronistic vibration, that slowly deteriorates the inner and outer life. Dependency on the substance only increases, leading the body closer to death.

People can also be used to fill a void. I suppose we can all relate to moments in our lives when we have experienced a crush on a guy or a gal. This person can often be a replacement object to symbolically fill the gap once given us by a primary caretaker (Winnicott, 1969). It is a sad day when the child realizes that she can't depend on her parents for certain kinds of love and attention and won't ever become that shining star in their eyes. This day comes when one realizes they must turn their attention outward into the world and try to find an outside love interest. We all go through a variation of this drama in some degree.

How smoothly that goes for us determines the magnitude of our needs and desires from others. Some children leave the nest more hurt, rejected, overstimulated, and angrier than others. All of this gets played out in relationships with other people.

It is helpful to be curious about your own relationship needs and patterns as you continue down the path and seek to develop emotional intimacies in this lifetime.

Take a moment to sit back and conjure up a memory of a time when you had a crush on another person. Whatever your memory is, I'm sure it will remind you just how illogical emotions sometimes are. They can even get so triggered that they take on a life of their own. Many of us have been obsessed with someone to some degree. On the subtle end of the spectrum, it can look like a mild crush; on the more extreme end, it mirrors addiction. This person who becomes obsessed eventually become truly devastated and convinced they've lost their last chance at happiness.

To get a better perspective on this, continue to look at yourself. Spend some quiet moments in mindful contemplation, holding the sensations of this experience (the crush) in your awareness. This way, you can use a typically harmless form of obsession to better understand the inner workings of obsession.

What does obsession look like? Many times, your mind has a thought, your mind believes that thought, your mind attaches a story to that thought, and the story becomes very meaningful. This cycle actually gives your mind a rest from anxiety. Illusion becomes a self-soothing tactic, whether you are aware of it or not. At least in your fantasy and fixation, you get soothing. Unconsciously, you can fall into a whole set of powerful feelings for another person, yet they are grossly out of proportion to what is actually happening in real life. Of course, just like there are infinite shades of love, there are just as many expressions of obsession.

These intense crushes that lead to obsessive, repetitive thoughts, fantasies, and actions can start for a variety of reasons. Again, it could be that the person somehow triggered a symbolic fantasy in your mind that allows you to experience an emotion that you have been craving.

Perhaps you fear abandonment and rejection, and this person is just warm and open toward you in a way that makes you feel safe and heard. You might fall into obsessively thinking about them and even searching for clues to prove they feel the same way for you.

How does obsession happen? Sometimes you can begin to idolize someone because they have character traits, talents, physical appearance, or something else you wish you had. A crush sprouts into a variation of obsession, which can continue for different reasons: you feel better about yourself when you are near them, you think about them constantly when you are left alone, you stalk them on social media as often as you can, you want to be the person or take on the person's persona, or you dream of experiencing the bliss-filled paradise with them constantly. You might have a Pygmalion fantasy that they will make you feel powerful or be your little project. These examples are early forms of obsession.

An obsession is a repetitive thought, idea, image, or urge about another person, or thing. That thought becomes something you experience as invasive. It consumes you and often leads you to feeling depleted, fearful, distressed, or uncomfortable. Obsession often leads to feeling like you will never be happy again. It can become a dark, insidious place. This delusion is very real for the obsessed.

How can obsession effect you? Obsession can actually handicap your life by taking such a hold on you that it clouds your choices and ability to move, expand, and interact in the world. Obsession can spin so far out of control that it may evolve into an addiction. The mind is a tricky and often slippery slope when emotions are heightened. A person's obsession can impede their getting to work, cause problems to their financial stability, or ruin their reputation. An obsession can stop a person from doing simple tasks like taking care of themselves, eating properly, or sleeping soundly. A person may slide into an isolated existence, letting go of other relationships or turning their backs on people in their lives, especially those who don't agree or oppose their obsession with their chosen object. When a person goes so far past rational thought, they may find themselves unable to stop antisocial and self-destructive behaviors. They may be stuck with craving attention from the other person in any way they can get it.

When an obsessed person loses the ability to function normally, it has become a serious, multidimensional problem that must be looked at with deep introspection and realization.

Object of Desire

Some of us may know what it feels like to be the object of someone's obsession, where someone has exhibited obsessive behavior toward you. Most often, we experience a person behaving in an irrational and destructive behavior toward us and lash out aggressively when the issue is presented as a projection. We might not say this, but ultimately the obsessed is stuck in self-hatred or has a desperate need to feel alive.

When you are the object, it is likely difficult to remain compassionate. In fact, empathy may fuel the obsessed into thinking they are receiving clues that you are returning the feelings they have for you. As the object of desire or aggression, you must objectively realize the person is suffering from an addiction. For the most part, obsessive and delusional thinking is looked at as a weakness by others, and people often turn their backs on the person. When parsing out your own feelings over their behavior, try to remember that they are unwell and need help. It can be scary when an obsession becomes criminal. They may turn to breaking the law or trying to disrupt your personal life through bullying or stalking to feel better about themselves.

The main thing to remember is that the person isn't even really seeing you. They are creating an illusion in their minds around who you are, what you symbolize for them, and how that feeds their ability to exist. Most of the time, an obsessed person has trouble respecting your personal space, and this is frustrating and scary. Most of the time, the best thing we can do as the object is create healthy boundaries with the person. If we have to see them in professional or personal circumstances, try to remain an even-keeled, detached, nonconfrontational, and lightly compassionate presence. Their happiness is not contingent upon you. Giving in to manipulations, or threats that they will destroy themselves if you leave them or don't return their feelings only enables their illness and hurts you.

Addictions and obsessions are very hard to overcome. Many people experience such deep self-hatred that this healing process is difficult to do alone. Often, it takes one person talking to another who understands them and a lot of abstinence and introspection.

How can we be with ourselves more so we can bond with ourselves more? Ultimately, the only relationship is with yourself, and that is always our focus. Sometimes it takes another person to help us see the beauty in ourselves.

The human personality is not the source of absolute love. It comes through us naturally when we fully open to ourselves: Sometimes this happens when another person shows us that we are acceptable, and worthy of understanding, of listening to, of exploring. Receiving pure love, caring, and recognition from another confers a great blessing. When the value and beauty of our existence is recognized, when we experience this kind of openness and warmth coming from another, it provides an essential nourishment. It affirms us in our being who we are, allowing us to say yes to ourselves. This allows us to relax, let go of tension, settle in to ourselves. It helps us experience our own warmth and openness, allowing us to recognize the beauty and goodness at the core of our nature. The light of unconditional love awakens the dormant seed potentials within us, helping them ripen, blossom, and bear fruit, to bring forth the unique gifts that are our offering to this Life. This opening makes us transparent to the life flowing through us, like a fresh breeze that enters a room as soon as the windows are raised.

—Osho

Turning Inward through the Acceptance of Another

Recently, a few days after I worked with a person for the first time, they wrote me an email:

> Hi, I went home and realized over the night and when I woke up that during our session, I had a new feeling. I couldn't figure out what it was. I realized when I woke up it was that I felt accepted. It may sound weird, but during our talk, I experienced an unconditional acceptance from you. Like you were welcoming all of me, I guess my essential nature. I can't recall a time when I have felt this before. The way you listened to me and the understanding you showed me made me feel open, vibrant, stronger in my true self. I felt a

joyful flowing when I went back into the world and went back to work. I long for this experience every day, and yet when I realized a day after that the feeling was fading, I felt a strong pull to come back to you for another meeting right away, to get the feeling back. I felt this strong urge to call you but feared that if I continue, I may become addicted to you and our time together. I crave this feeling of being completely, unconditionally accepted so deeply because I feel that it nourishes my soul and makes me feel very alive. I fear that I have no concept for how to feel it without you because I have never felt it before.

I replied:

I am very happy for you having had this experience of unconditional love and acceptance. In my experience, it is love you felt from within, through what you were feeling from me, that allowed your essential self to shine through. Not to worry. What we do here in session is allow you to experience this internal connection to yourself, to have that unconditional acceptance of yourself, through feeling it from me. That is our focus here. I help you feel it and then gradually teach you to find that experience within yourself, through learning to meditate on experiencing your mind and body, understand and accept your feelings, your thoughts, and aspirations. Ultimately, you wouldn't have been able to have that experience through me if part of you didn't already feel acceptance and love toward yourself! Together, we are inviting and empowering this connection to absolute source that already resides within you. The limitless expansion you describe is that connection, an interconnection between your mind and body, and then a spiritual vibrancy with all living beings, beyond your material form. When we were talking, you learned to attune to, be with, and channel yourself by connecting within.

This person expressed surprise by my response.

Can you help me experience this kind of self-love and acceptance on my own? I would be eternally grateful.

Our continued talks inspired me to share this because it directly relates to the fear born through first feeling self-love through the acceptance from another. Most people feel fear in this circumstance because it is new, and if they become attached to a person, they fear losing a part of themselves. In careful guidance and therapeutic care, you will be led to find the ability to love and accept yourself. This happens first through the mirror of the other and practicing and new ways of relating to yourself, emotionally and physically.

Internal Riches

We often experience ourselves through the eyes of the other, but true happiness is never contingent upon one person or relationship. The best way to find true union with others is to find union with yourself.

Look within. What blocks you from source? Often what blocks us is also our greatest inspiration. When used to fill a void, the defense blocks union with source. When the defense is identified as a communication, it becomes a way to understand your desires and intentions. There, the block can fuel union.

To truly listen within, we must depart from linear thinking, time-lines, goals, and success measured on performance or how others receive us. We must understand that thought and time are the same. If you have a thought, you are in time. You need to know how to enter the cracks between thoughts. You can settle into a timeless, placeless world where you enter the nature of your mind. This is beyond the chattering mind, the anxious mind, the internal dialogue, and where you can enter emptiness. Clarity speaks through this space. Just as plants have spontaneous wisdom toward life growth and libidinal force, you do as well.

As we seek to discover a spiritual awareness, planted as a trust at the core of our intentions and perspectives, we need to discover the cause of the disturbance. We need to tune in and accept what we are experiencing and feeling. Learn to calm through acceptance and then sustain that focus on the stillness between the thoughts in your mind. Here are the riches. Here, we begin to truly listen to ourselves and understand our inner needs, desires, and conflicts.

We must learn to understand when mental cognition helps and when it pulls us away from being able to exist in pure openness. We must learn that we have a choice. You can learn to focus your mind on cognition when you need it and let it go when you don't. Allow stillness, openness be the place you consistently return to. Eventually it will be a part of your being—even in a very focused, high-stress environment. This peaceful interior throughout all you do is called serenity. You cultivate true, sustainable glory, pride, and riches through becoming present and satisfied in the moment. This has nothing to do with how much you have or don't have.

Let's all be externally successful and internally wealthy. This is what the life force wants. We are not meant to have to choose: poor but happy, rich and unhappy, unloved but rich, or poor but loved. We can be successful, rich, and empathetic and live a life of absolute love.

True Confidence

True confidence resides in feeling connected to mind, body, heart, and source. We need to learn to allow ourselves to be with our feelings, gently, paying close and compassionate attention. This simple gift of giving ourselves a chance to be heard by ourselves opens wellsprings of spontaneous healing. Here, the inner tantrum we may be experiencing through anxiety due to defenses against internal feelings and conflict suddenly quiets. Here, our negative thoughts calm some, and here, we can really tune in to our feelings.

When strong emotions or negative thoughts arise, the best thing to do is drop into the body and figure out how you feel. As you find the time and space to slow down and reflect, you will learn more about how your own thoughts, feelings, and emotions all work together. If you stay stuck in suppressing because you fear your response to them, or feel they will overwhelm you, you will remain stuck in patterns rather than learning something new about yourself.

Let's continue to train ourselves to drop into feeling our bodies. Continue to open the space within by expanding breath and tune in to feeling your heart. Listening to your heartbeat can help you return to confidence through your relationship to your internal self. Here resides true wealth. We do this by first seeking true confidence by getting to know our internal selves and making a daily practice of connecting to mind, body, heart, and source. Accepting and feeling the desires in you now will lead you to experiencing internal chemical bonding and expansion of heart. Acceptance and awareness ease tension and anxiety.

Cultivating true source of spirit through mind-body-heart connection will bring out the aspects of us that are more interested in joys, being with and there for nourishing friendships, becoming empathetic and present parents, caring people—and ultimately, more satisfied in all parts of our lives.

Mindfulness
Journaling Practice 6
Anxiety

Write down your thoughts and feelings often. Getting ideas out of the mind gives a feeling of relief, and seeing them written down gives opportunities to consider objectively later on. Be gentle with yourself and begin to learn yourself.

Free-Floating Anxiety

Think about what creates the most anxiety in your life. What am I experiencing viscerally now? What causes anxiety in my life? What do I feel when I think of the unknowns in my future? The world? How does anxiety feel in my body? Where? How does my mind react? What am I yearning for in those moments? Do I calm this dis-ease with a substance or quick fix? Do I want to understand myself better? What do I say to myself when I feel anxious? Am I conflicted over feelings and trying to push them away? It is normal to have many different feelings in one circumstance. Trying to get yourself to decide on one feeling is a way to avoid the confusing palette. Try to listen to all of them.

Negative Self-Talk

What are the repetitive thoughts in my mind? Can I quiet my mind and direct it toward feeling the sensations in my body? What do I feel physiologically? What is the mind chatter trying to communicate or defend against feeling? What does my body wisdom tell me? Can I pause to tune in to my body before making communications? Does my mind chatter occur at certain times of day or in certain circumstances? Can I learn to hear it, accept it, and let it go?

Persona and Masks

What do I truly want in my life? What am I afraid others will find out about me? What do I feel when I think of the unknowns of my future? The world? Do I look at my body as a machine, something that can help prove my validation in the world? Do I look at my body as something that is a very beautiful creation through which I can access a connection to life force? Do I see others in this same way? Can I look past their skin, their form, and see, feel inside of them the interconnection we share of life force and spirit?

Mindfulness
Meditation Practice 6
Spirit and Source

Sit or lie down. Find acceptance of where you are now. My voice is speaking to you. Through you. Listen to the quiet spaces between the thoughts in your mind. Feel your body. Listen to the wisdom your body is communicating. Listen to your defenses against feeling. Move back to focusing your mind on feeling. Try to locate the energy moving through your veins and cells. Actually try to feel its vibration and fluid movement like a stream pulsing though your being. Yes, this is a physiological sensation. It is also the groundwork for awareness of a spiritual force. Some say that this spiritual force of mysterious life is outside you. In mind-and-body union, we learn connection to source by revering the life force that is in you now. The resonating pulse of your natural life force energy—inside of you. This force pulses through all living beings, outside of you. We are all one and the same, within and without. There is no separation. This life force is constantly vibrating within all of us, all of life. This is a source of love that never exists without you. Resonate with the present moment. Resonate with your inner existence. This will give you peace and aliveness in your body, your mind, and your life, and you will exude love and confidence. The interconnectedness between the life force in your body and the life force in all other living things is profound, limitless, and infinite. We are not separate. You are in the center of the ocean, the heart of a deer, the volcano, and the elderly man on the

corner. Ultimately, on some energetic level, you feel all
of it now. Pulse. The only true intimacy to be found is in
your enlightenment. You are already enlightened. In the now.
It is an internal affair, in each of us. The divine union of our po-
larities. That is how we come to it. When we make love, we become
the loving. There is no question about what we are trying to get to or
achieve; it all melts away as we become the caressing. Through practicing, we become it. We don't surmount or overcome our obstacles.
We dissolve them so the inherent inner light can shine through. This
is the secret. Everything is changed by that one simple principle and
by the practices that stimulate the reality of it in the nervous system.
The suggestion is to redirect our desires toward wanting to unfold in
yourself. Then things will happen.

Chapter 7

Emotions and Your Heart

Absolute love is the love of being. What feels most affirming is not just to feel loved, but to feel loved as we are. "As we are" means: "in our very being." When we have a loving, understanding, and open relation to ourselves, our heart opens. When we focus on our heart, We open. We bloom. Our ability to accept ourselves opens to True Source. Manifesting a relationship to Source warms us from within, creating inner confidence, a sense of well-being, appreciation and joie de vivre. We are the channels through which this radiance flows. We have a natural wish to reach toward this deepest essence, our life's blood. We cannot help wanting to fill with this essential aspect of our nature.
—Osho

In this chapter, we will discuss the importance of a healthy heart-and-mind connection. I will describe the role of your thymus gland in this harmony. Positive emotion practices will help you heal from negative thought patterns that induce anxiety and move into a happy mind-body-heart union. At the close of this chapter, journaling and meditation practices will help you develop positive perspectives and a peaceful ease in your mind and body.

Emotions in Your Body

As we have been discussing, your emotions originate in your body and brain. Let's also look at the relationship between your heart and brain. Your heart is one of the main healing forces in your body and mind. Certain practices can help you consciously open your heart.

Your heart is a magnificent, essential, divine source for your life.

Your heart is consistently working to supply a pulse of oxygenated blood throughout your body. You would not be able to survive if it suddenly decided to stop. Your heart also graces your total emotional landscape. Your heart has a constant two-way dialogue with your brain.

I have read and watched research studies dedicated to understanding the interrelationship between your heart and the physiology of your emotions. It is easy to see how the heart and emotions are linked and how we can shift the heart into a more efficient state by monitoring its rhythms.

This is one specific study I want to share with you. Scientists monitored people's heartbeats and brains while they were telling emotional stories from their personal lives. They monitored them again while the people were listening to other people's emotional stories. The research showed that, of all the bodily organs, the heart is a center where we experience many of our feelings—from a quickening beat when you see a loved one after a long separation to a painful moment, like a pain in the heart or heartache when you hear bad news. These kinds of occurrences create a physiological counterpart in the body that most people have experienced. Both tests showed similar patterns of activation in the insular cortex—the same location in the brain that is involved in interoception and emotions. Interoception is a kind of internal perception!

According to these studies, when your body sends emotional communication to your brain, your brain sends signals specifically back to your heart. In fact, your heart sends more information to the brain than the brain sends to the heart, and your brain responds to your heart in many important ways. There is a very intimate relationship between your emotion and your heart. We have been provided new scientific insight into understanding how the activity of your heart is linked to your emotions, health, vitality, and well-being. Emotions create a chain reaction in the body. As you read, reflect on your own mind-body-heart connection in relationship to your life experiences.

First, when we experience feelings like irritation, anger, frustration, anxiety, or insecurity, the heart's rhythm patterns become more erratic. These erratic patterns affect the nervous system and are sent to the emotional centers in the brain. The brain recognizes the erratic heart patterns as negative or stressful feelings, and your stress hormone levels increase. Your blood vessels respond by constricting, which makes your blood pressure rise. Due to this constriction in positive, nutrient-rich blood circulating throughout your body, the immune system weakens. These erratic heart rhythms also block your ability to think clearly. Your brain goes into stress mode. Chemical overdrive creates fuzzy thoughts or dislocates links between different parts of the brain. If you consistently experience challenging emotions, it can put a long-term strain on your heart and other organs, and it often amplifies the risk of heart disease and other significant health problems.

The resonation of emotion actually happens through the brain, heart, and body acting in concert. Your heart responds to your emotional and mental reactions. Certain emotions stress the body and drain our energy, and other emotions give us energy and a feeling of well-being.

When you experience heartfelt emotions like love, care, appreciation, and compassion, your heart produces a very different rhythm. In this case, it is a smooth pattern that looks like gently rolling hills. Harmonious heart rhythms, which reflect positive emotions, are considered indicators of cardiovascular efficiency and nervous system balance. This lets your brain know that its intimate friend, the heart, feels good and often creates a gentle, warm feeling in your heart.

Good news! You are not enslaved by your emotions. In fact, wallowing for extended periods of time in painful emotions can be detrimental to your health. Certainly, it is important to allow ourselves to feel all of our feelings. Seeking a "spiritual bypass" or "shoulding" on ourselves to feel differently than we do stresses the mind-body connection. On the other hand, feeling acceptance of our internal selves and our feelings orchestrates a calming circulation of truth in our being. Undoubtedly, all the feelings we try to push away need to be expressed and will inevitably come out sideways. Feelings don't always need to be acted out; they can be accepted, fantasized, and expressed in varying ways. Wallowing in them will only create health problems due to the strain it puts on your heart and nervous system.

As we move along, I will suggest some positive emotion exercises to help you move out of negative pitfalls and back into heart-centered love.

Thymus Gland

Your thymus gland is a lymphatic organ that is located just beneath your breastbone, aligned with your heart. It is responsible for the creation of T-cells during maturation, making it crucial in the development of your immune system. Your thymus gland begins to decrease in size after you go through puberty, declining to about 15 percent of its original form by the time you reach fifty, especially if a lot of toxins and stress-related chemicals are pulsing through your body. Because of its direct relationship to immunity, your thymus is the chief executive of how quickly you age. A healthy and calm heart creates a person with more vital energy, and youthfulness. And if you do become ill, you will be able to heal more quickly than if your heart is tight and closed.

The way you treat your body is an important part of having a healthy heart and mind. Your heart health is directly related to the health of your cardiovascular system, lung health, and thymus gland.

- ✺ Your natural energetic circulation and flow are significantly affected by the amount of water you drink and healthy, clean, and light food you consume.
- ✺ Exercise allows your body to generate positive chemistry like endorphins, serotonin, and oxytocin, which calm and enliven the nervous system.
- ✺ Sleep helps the nervous system rejuvenate and your heart beat more calmly. This helps create an ability to breathe more calmly and cleanse toxins from your body more efficiently.
- ✺ A healthy emotional state is important for maintaining heart health. Positive emotion-focused practices also help reduce

stress and anxiety, which is a safe and effective way to lower blood pressure and increase the functional capacity in your heart. Some types of positive emotion practices are currently being used in hospitals and cardiac rehabilitation programs around the country.

An appreciative heart is good medicine. It is healthy to learn to shift lovingly and gently as a form of self-care—out of stressful emotional reactions and into heartfelt emotions. This can have profound positive effects on your cardiovascular system and your overall mental and physical health and quality of life.

Focused practices that enhance positive emotions can help you replace stressful emotional patterns and perceptions you may have developed as your familiar way of being with new patterns based in positive perceptions and emotions.

Practice Appreciation

Appreciation is one of the most concrete and easiest positive emotions for you to self-generate and sustain for longer periods. It is centered on your perceptions, how you choose to view circumstances, and what you choose to focus on. If you choose to see the positive aspects in your circumstances and appreciate the totality of what you are experiencing, even if some aspects are uncomfortable, you will find new perspectives and opportunities for growth and choice.

One of the long-term benefits of the practice of positive emotion and perspective is increased emotional awareness. This increased awareness can help you maintain a more consistent emotional balance since you are no longer a slave to your learned reactions and familiar ways of relating to yourself and the world. You will also improve your cardiovascular health, lung health, and thymus gland functioning. The more joy you radiate, the longer you will want to live! I am here to help you learn to shift your emotional state from fear-based response to heart-led action by helping you find ways to listen more closely to your heart.

Open Your Heart

Put your mind's eye (like we do with interoception) inside your heart. Imagine that your heart muscles are relaxing. Often, we hold tension and anxiety in the heart, and it stops the flow of natural body chemistry like oxytocin to move in and out of your heart center. This stops you from being able to receive the energy of love and feel it flow from inside of you outward.

When your heart is open, you will freely give and receive both romantic and unconditional love. If having a commitment to another person is something you want in your life, and your heart is open, you will be able to do this because having an open heart enables you to forgive hurts and extend much more compassion to people by trying to understand where they are coming from rather than judging or running away. This will allow you to give and receive intimacy with more depth of understanding in both yourself and the other, which will make you more trustworthy and reliable and give you a deeper capacity for commitment.

You will be more richly aware of the present moment by being able to drop into your senses more. You will be in touch with your feelings, both positive and negative, and your relationships will be of higher priority for you. You will find happiness whatever the circumstances of your life because you will have a grounded sense of belonging on this earth and accepting the natural flow of your life's events. You will be able to laugh more frequently and share your joy with others and with yourself. You will experience loving, intimate relationships and moments of sexual ecstasy with your partner because you will be that open. You will look at your life with more focus on gratitude for what you have and the beauty that is within and surrounds you.

When you are living with a closed heart, you will also have great difficulty communicating in relationships. You will shut down your feelings. You might become dull and predictable. You might feel alone a lot or move from one relationship to another. When closed, you may find yourself using thinking, reason, and intellect for your refuge. You might become a workaholic, working constantly to get away from experiencing people, and look at your life as half empty rather than half full.

When your heart is closed, you may find that you aren't inspired to take care of your health. You might grieve for many months or years over something, and if you get sick, you may heal very slowly.

Shift Your Mental Perspective

It is easy to fall into a negative perspective or outlook. When the mind is filled with negative projections and thoughts, we become enshrouded in an expectation that the world or people involved with your circumstances are looking to hurt you or take from you. This can lead to suspicions, assumptions, rejection, and negatively charged relationships. Perhaps this is your mind protecting you from people who are not looking out for your best interest, but let's not jump to assuming the worst.

Feelings are not always facts. First, try to look at the circumstance from a different point of view. Try to see the circumstance from many different perspectives and see the positives you are experiencing in the circumstance and not just the negatives. See if there is something you can do to take responsibility for the circumstance and shift your behavior. See if there is something you need to communicate, and if so, find a way to do it constructively and with the intention of creating a deeper bond of love and union.

Stay Connected to Your Body

There is always enough love to go around because love is always within you if you learn to cultivate it. However, it is easy to become disconnected from your body throughout the day, especially in this culture since we have been taught to be cerebrally led instead of heart and body led. As we all know, that often leads to a diseased life—a life of chemicals, covering up emotions, cancer or physical illness, prescription medications, and substances to feel better. A life of abusing people and abusing ourselves. When we are moving toward shutting down, our hearts are closed. We feel stuck in a fear-based existence. We don't need to live that way. Luckily, there is never a shortage of love in the world.

This practice of attuning to the life force circulation in your body allows your anxiety to rest and your nervous system to find the balance and trust that allows you to live with confidence. As you develop a deeper connection to source through your mind-and-body union, your heart opens.

Focus on Love

Love, the experience of love from within and shared loved, generates many wonderful natural chemicals in our bodies, like oxytocin, serotonin, and endorphins. This accelerates natural cell growth in your body and brain and stimulates circulation flow. Here, inspiration, libidinal drive, and creativity expand. Here, we prosper. We are alive and growing rather than shutting down and deteriorating!

Through this way of resonating with yourself, you actively become more open to experiencing deeper reservoirs of love and experience a natural ability to resonate with others. Within this wellspring of interconnected life force is a wisdom that pulses. You actively begin to feel and observe empathy. Herein lies the ability to have a choice between living a life grounded in fear-based reactions and making choices to slow down, feel your feelings, find truth, and choose heart-led actions and responses. When your heart is open, you are able to let go of protecting your internal self with a need to separate, compare, defend, project, or create a persona. By resonating with your own heart, an open, balanced nervous system, you will naturally resonate with the people you are interacting with. Here, your state of conscious empathetic awareness of them, yourself, and universal consciousness will be united.

Empathy

Empathy is a gift. Empathy allows us the ability to resonate with and learn from each person rather than judging or pushing people or ourselves away. When we are in an open-hearted, empathic resonance, we are able to experience the feelings, the intimacy aroused between us, through the mirror that others present. The feelings you experience through heart-led intimacy with others are your greatest teachers. You can seek to understand, learn, and grow from the experiences you are gifted by remaining empathetic toward yourself and others.

Slow Down and Trust the Universal Consciousness

People often say, "The spirit speaks through people." Love does not always look like or arrive in the package we expect it to. Love and empathy are feelings. The arrival of them does not have to be based on the conditions of a specific circumstance. Resonating in love and empathy can arouse many different feelings and surface in many different ways. Life is not about chasing after love or acting like you feel it when you don't just because the situation looks good. Love can be your greatest teacher. It is not always a totally soothing, pleasurable comfort. Empathy often creates a mirror resonance between you and others. This is beautiful for learning about yourself and developing emotional maturity. When you choose to live this kind of heart-led existence, you will transform the energy of your emotions in profound ways.

The exercises that follow provide guidance for how to lead a more empathetic life.

Have you ever read the prayer of St. Francis of Assisi? It is a lovely way to slow down, find your heart center, and remind yourself of the healing powers of empathy and forgiveness.

> Make me an instrument of your peace; where there is
> hatred, let me sow love; where there is injury, pardon;

where there is discord, union; where there is doubt, faith; where there is despair, hope; where there is darkness, light; and where there is sadness, joy. Grant that I may not so much seek to be consoled, as to console; to be understood, as to understand; to be loved, as to love; for it is in giving that we receive, it is in pardoning that we are pardoned, and it is in dying that we are born to eternal life.

You will grow exponentially more than you ever will if you remain caught up in resentment, comparison, envy, greed, fear, and rejection. When comparing, feeling you are hateful, unable to see your part, feel the other, communicate lovingly, learn from your feelings and experiences. You remain rigid, unable to flow, grow, and live a healthy, cellular balance. This begins inside of you.

Slow down. Focus on beginning to learn what the resonation of love feels like in your body. By focusing on the feeling of love in your body and heart, you naturally generate more of it. Focusing your mind on anything makes it expand. Let love move in and out of you through the giving and receiving of love.

Mindfulness
Journaling Practice 7

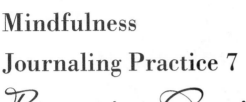

Becoming Curious

Simply sit and write out a few thoughts and feelings as you read through this. A little whisper from me: "You deserve to feel safe, listened to, and taken care of in this world. This begins with you listening to you, taking care of you, and making choices that are healthy and safe for you in your life."

Let's get to know you!

What do I enjoy doing with my time? Where does my mind wander when I am alone? Are they negative thoughts? How does my body respond? Can I direct myself to seeing the positives in the circumstances? How does my body respond? What do I get out of focusing on the negative? What do I get out of focusing on the positive? How does my heart respond to doing things I love to do? Do I do these things often or stop myself? What brings me most tension? Most freedom? Where is my favorite place in nature?

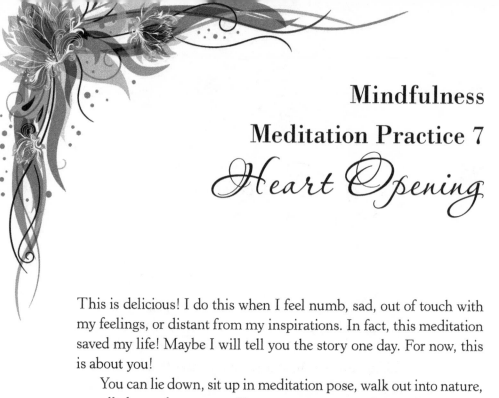

Mindfulness
Meditation Practice 7
Heart Opening

This is delicious! I do this when I feel numb, sad, out of touch with my feelings, or distant from my inspirations. In fact, this meditation saved my life! Maybe I will tell you the story one day. For now, this is about you!

You can lie down, sit up in meditation pose, walk out into nature, or walk down a busy street. You can attune to your heart wherever you are. It is a beautiful mindfulness heart practice.

Find your breath and experience the movement of your lungs, ribs, center, and pelvis as you deepen and expand your breath. As you exhale, feel the heat, the sensations of air flowing throughout your body. Your breath acts as an internal massage. Become aware of the beating of your own heart. Listen to this beautiful, profound instrument and all of its magical reverberations throughout your being. When you tune in to the simple, visceral, and profoundly powerful beating of your own heart, you will notice a warmth passing through your body and mind. You might think, *Wow, I haven't felt my heart in a long time! Wow, my heartbeat is fast. Let me soothe myself by slowing it down to a consistent rhythm through my mind focus and breath.*

As you tune in to listening to this magnificent beating of your own heart, imagine that pulsing through its vibration is an emerald green ripple, glistening in the sunlight on the surface of the sea. As you listen to the beating of your heart, feel this effervescent ripple moving, gyrating, pulsing, and radiating inside of each cell and chamber of your heart.

As the ripple in your heart continues to pulse, imagine and sense its ability for limitless expansion. Begin to imagine your heartbeat is growing, shedding its individuality as a single ripple, and dancing, spiraling, intertwining, melding with the ripples, vibrations, and sunbeams beside it. Feel the depths of your heartbeat, the reverberation inside of your chest, your lungs, your thymus gland, throughout the pulse of your entire body. Feel your heart beating in your wrists, your ankles, your neck, your stomach, your pelvis. Continue to feel that ripple moving throughout the mysterious and deep emerald seas, out into the ethers, the entire universe, galaxies. Suddenly, you, this beating heart, this vibrating and moving ripple, feel at one with the depth of the ocean, and you feel interconnected with every other ripple and vibration in nature, in the universe, inside of the blazing sun, deep into the core magma at the center of the earth. You feel a connectedness with the totality of source. With this awareness, guide yourself, your heart, to recognizes every other ripple or person as an expression of that. Imagine you are interconnected and at ease with every other energetic source, people, animals, tree, and parallel universes. You are beyond material form. You are at ease and in a calm, serene bliss with other people.

As you expand this awareness of your heart's capacity for divine love, experiencing its powerful beating and central warmth, listen to the intuitive thoughts that enter your mind, seeking to understand your feelings, let them move through your being without fear or defenses. Then slowly, as you allow yourself to experience the profundity of all of life around and within us, open your mind to focus on the aspects of your life you are most appreciative of, enlightening your mind, body, heart, and spirit by seeking and welcoming positive thoughts, wellsprings of emerald light into your heart.

Focus on these positive feelings of gratitude and appreciation.

Allow them to grow larger, spreading throughout all the ripples in the universe. Focus on the feelings of positivity inside of you and send them into the center of source, all energetic flow in the universe, imagining and knowing you can help fortify this source and send your positivity back into the rest of the ripples simply by sharing your appreciation, letting it energetically meld with the vibrations that create libidinal flow throughout all. Finding yourself counting your blessings, begin to send blessings and appreciations, warmth, emerald rays and ripples, prayers, or good intention to each person you love. And then become so filled with light that you feel able to send good feelings, prayers, appreciations to those people you are holding resentments against. Resentments are a powerful poison in your body, creating stress, toxins, and illness. Sending prayers to those you resent is a powerful way to calm your anxieties and open your heart. It will help you have a more open heart, more compassion for yourself and others, and more connection to the divine source within us all.

Don't judge yourself if it is difficult to find something to appreciate. Maybe you feel exceptionally knotted up today or in general in your life. You are here to learn—not to be perfect. There are many reasons why a person may initially find it difficult to self-generate a feeling of appreciation in the present moment. You are allowed to feel whatever you feel. The first step toward transformation is acceptance of what is. Almost anyone can find something to genuinely appreciate.

Try to recall a memory or conjure up a fantasy that elicits warm feelings in you. By simply recalling a time when you felt sincere appreciation and recreating that feeling or fantasizing about a dream come true or some beautiful happening, you can increase your heart rhythm coherence, relax your nervous system, and improve your health. With practice and patience, most people are able to self-generate feelings of appreciation in the present and no longer need the past time reference.

It is not the mental image of a memory or fantasy that creates this shift in your heart rhythm; it is the emotions associated with the memory. Mental images do not produce the result of positive radiance alone.

You must allow yourself to focus on a positive feeling. Focus on the pleasure sensations and feel them reverberating throughout your body, heart, and mind and into the universe.

By focusing on this heart opening and practicing to circulate pleasure sensation in your body, you can increase your own pleasure and passion throughout all you do. The focus is on understanding how your sensual and loving energy, also known as "pure desire," are one.

Healthy pleasure is the genuine spirit of humankind. This is thought of as the natural self, and feeling the limitless love within leads to healing trauma, mind-body union, self-realization, and even nirvana. Traditionally, the body and mind should be prepared by healthy physical exercise, diet, breathing exercises (pranayama), sensory-based meditation, and expanding positive feelings like appreciating, honoring, protecting, and adoring your mind and body.

As you concentrate on opening your heart, allow the power of that pure love light to shine forth from within. You can give so much more freely with joy. You can begin to find spiritual worship through the experiences that meditative or trancelike states stimulate via the electrical activity of your brain.

Food for Thought!

A common theme in sexual passion and spiritual illumination is love. This common theme of love being both spiritual and sexual is not coincidental. It reflects an underlying link that prehistoric civilizations intuited and modern science is now beginning to rediscover. We have been taught that human sexuality, which is in essence a striving for connection or oneness with and through another to a greater life force, and the emotion of love, which is us striving for connection or oneness, with another and then to a greater life force, and a spiritual striving for a spiritual union or oneness with what we call the divine in worship—wherever you go to worship or however you worship—the striving for union or oneness with the divine is spiritual. We have been taught that these experiences are all completely different from one another. Sexual love, emotional love, and spiritual divinity love are all different from one another, but they are all striving for the same thing: a connection, a union.

This is what happens in our bodies that brings on a spiritual or trancelike state.

Think about your sexual experiences. Have you experienced sexual interconnection with your heart during self-touch? During lovemaking? Do you feel you need to close your heart when you self-touch or make love? Has the act of lovemaking ever felt like a meditation, a prolonged state of expanded consciousness? These states of meditation rejuvenate your circulatory system, body chemistry, brain activity, thymus gland, adrenal gland circulations, and overall positivity and vitality. What are your thoughts and experiences with this idea?

Chapter 8
Soul Evolution

In this chapter, we will learn how to analyze psychological repetitions. I will discuss the seven deadly sins as a means to interpret when you are using adaptive survival mechanisms as a means for self-destruction or positive growth. We will explore philosophical concepts around truth and inevitable change. At the close of this chapter, journaling and meditation practices will help you understand how to listen more deeply to your inner truth, heart, and soul. These concepts are core elements in letting go of repetitive traumatic stories and realizing total presence in your mind, body, and soul.

Soul-Conscious Evolution

Today we are going to discuss something of a more esoteric nature: soul-conscious evolution. The concept of soul evolution is about your energetic transformational capabilities on this plane, your quest for ultimate truth. I simply ask you to open your mind and explore your relationship to these concepts.

In Dr. Henry Grayson's *Use Your Body to Heal Your Mind*, he says,

> It's consciousness that rules. That's the message we get from worldwide spiritual wisdom and what's emerging more in quantum physics as well. It's really consciousness that rules, not matter. If we're trying to heal the body without healing the mind, using the mind to heal the body, we missed the basic healing

that's necessary for us. We need to heal the mind
that may have even needed the body to be sick, or
the thought that it could be sick, that was told it was
vulnerable, that it had to be a victim of this or that
germ or event, but to recognize that consciousness is
the issue, we take back our power and find our true
self in the process, then the body just naturally heals
in response to that.

To me, humans are big walking receivers, taking in experience through
our senses, processing it in our minds and bodies, and expressing it
in our actions. Yes, my favorite. Energy never dies; it is continuously
transforming. We are energetic beings mostly comprised of vibrations
that are seeking synchronicity and balance, always evolving, transforming, and transmuting energy. This may be a letdown to you if you
are not aligned with the magnitude of this kind of universal legacy,
which transcends personal DNA lineage, but transforming energy is
really all we are ever doing. We can trust and rely on that. We may
not know how it will happen, but we are given tools and techniques to
continue to explore ways to access potential, channel, release, express,
and transmute energy.

The ultimate goal in this Karma cycle is for the soul to progress to
the highest level of existence: become one with the universe. Soul evolution naturally occurs when something happens in one's life to cause
them to refocus and feel the need to reach deep within and reflect
on how to live. Soul evolution leads persons to different and higher
pathways of life. One is compelled to visit sacred sites, seek master
instructors, and find insight. Soul evolution promotes energy and the
intention required to transform. Soul evolution provides one with
universal actions that are embraced. Spiritual alignment is achieved
through innermost truth. Soul evolution brings one to a higher state
of hope, faith, and love.

All levels of consciousness, whether they are human, spirit, or
atomic in form, exist within a continuum. All things move and churn
in their own cosmos, within their own realm of reality and within

their own perception of god/goddess, male/female, or human/animal form. We are speaking on the energetic level of all consciousness whether physical or not; everything around you, every being's experience and any observation made by any level of consciousness is a matter of perception.

Everything you do, have done, or will do is also a matter of perception: your own perception. Others see your actions within the realm of your own perception, and there is no true beginning of the evolution of consciousness. You have and always will perceive in your own manner within the room of god or goddess or universal life force. Your soul is a great tool of observation. It gains experience and gives to the whole in every movement. Your choices are the fundamental acts you perform in your journey of collecting information, and you experience life using your own, unique manner of perception.

There are multiple realities, and you are right now perceiving reality as only you can perceive because your soul travels with group energy. You happen to be at this time experiencing reality with a group of souls who have similar methods of perception and gathering experiences. The cosmos beyond the physical universe is vast, endless, and timeless. Being such, there are levels and varieties of consciousness that do not in any way perceive the way that you do. There is absolutely no similarity whatsoever in perceptions. However, it can be said as well that on your own sphere, there are levels of consciousness that do not in any way perceive the world that you do. A cell in the blade of grass, a candle flame, an insect, and a drop of water all have a different method of perceiving their universe.

Your own perceptions are truly and wonderfully important for your soul's evolution, but they are by no means the truth, the whole truth, and nothing but the truth. In fact, truth, being, and living in truth are only matters of perception. What is your reality may not be another's reality. The reason you experience kinship next to or with another soul or souls is that you have similar methods of perception. Therefore, you can exist here on a mass level semi-harmoniously, in general agreement of how things are supposed to be.

On a more intimate level, you live only near those who share your current perception of life and reality, and you socialize with those who harmoniously support your perceptions as your perceptions change, your associates change, or your jobs change. You always gravitate toward those who share your perceptions. Therefore, you have your earth here and all of the matter and the oceans and all of the people here who get it the way you get it. If you think there is a vast separation between your own reality and those who choose to live on your planet, in war, famine, violence, or poverty, then imagine the vast and explicable difference between your current perceptions and those on other planes and dimensions! Indescribable levels of masses of consciousness live beyond your sphere of multiple realities, and the greater amount never experience your earth or anything like it.

Consciousness is huge, vast, whole, and inseparable, but the whole god, goddess, universal life force, whatever you call it, exists in realities and levels of perception that you cannot even imagine at this time. You travel on your path, your road of soul evolution, choosing and preferring different methods of collecting your preferred experiences. As you do so, you travel with groups of souls who choose similar methods of perception. Soul preference brings you together with like levels of consciousness, and you experience together and participate in each other's lessons.

Many of the great mystics of the past believed that each object or form of life on your planet is in complete agreement with the chosen reality of the earth's mass consciousness. Synchronicity is always present—even when it is hard to trust the orchestra of circumstances that we observe as our reality.

Look at your life. Are there things you feel especially attuned to? Are there people you don't always feel you resonate with? Are there people you feel you have a deep understanding with? Your soul is an energetic force that is comprised of life force energy. This life force holds the pattern of gravity and energies that keep the universe organized a natural flow.

Atoms and Molecules

We can get to a basic understanding of these concepts by looking at atomic structures and molecules. Orbiting structures of atoms that remain in attraction to one another and continue in a similar orbit. All matter is made up of these things, and you are material form comprised of just this. Your soul is an imprint of this life force energy, and it holds a certain vibrational force that gives you tendencies, interests, memories, resonances, and recollections of people and places that you cannot explain.

Look at your own experience in this lifetime now. When your body dies, your soul goes back into universal life force energy that makes up the universe's energetic holding pattern of light. When a person is born, parts of this soup separate and move into the body to live a life of combined spirit and matter to continue to learn lessons and evolve, eventually becoming reabsorbed into this life force light. This is the rule of karmic cycle.

Recognizing Patterns

Have you ever noticed the patterns in your life? Look at the dynamics between your parents and yourself. What interests did you take on naturally as a child? Have you repeated the same kinds of relationships or felt like you have been in the same cycle since you were a child? Often, we can only see the relationships between these patterns and how our parents taught us, how they related to one another and to us, how our siblings related to us, what we experienced growing up in relation to others, and how we reacted and responded. Maybe we can go back as far as our grandparents or great-grandparents and see the relationship between them and our parents and our parents and us.

Like genetic inheritances, psychological influences are passed down, which may create patterns or cycles we continue to live through, outlive, and create in our lives and for generations to come. We can look even more deeply and see that these are cycles the soul is going through. By learning new ways of doing things and taking different actions in the material plane, we can change the vibrational patterns of how and with whom we relate to as living beings in this world.

Since energy attracts like energy, we attract people and experiences that resonate on a similar wavelength with us, which is the normal way to define who we spend time with, how we meet, and what we do together. On a deeper level, we are drawn to people of vibrational patterning and output similar to ours. As we change our inner structuring, learn lessons, and revise our actions, we change who and what we resonate with on the outside.

Our energy and actions change, and we start to see the patterning in our own lives. We find opportunities to learn lessons from these experiences rather than just fighting against things, becoming frustrated, or blaming others or ourselves. We can learn from these influences. Everything that happens in life is a lesson. Everything that happens in life is an opportunity to create change, create a deeper awareness, allow ourselves a little more space for our soul to breathe, and experience a different awareness. Perhaps our bodies or our intentions could be led by a different action. This takes deep awareness and the yearning to truly be living a fully intentional, truth-inspired life rather than just going through the motions and living out the same patterns over and over again. It is our choice to begin to notice these patterns and make different choices.

Learning from Life

Let's talk about learning lessons from the things that happen in your life rather than fighting against them. The things that are presented to us in our lives are often meant as ways to teach us new things and allow us to grow, and we often don't choose to see it that way. Unfortunately, we choose to see that there is something wrong with us or with our lives, and we begin to compare ourselves to other people. We wonder why they have more and why their lives seem better, but there is really no such thing as someone having a better life! Your life is your destiny, and you can take actions. I am not suggesting you just live a course of life and accept whatever is given to you, but you can take actions with a true awareness of attention as attuned to your truth and take actions based on your integrity rather than just doing something to cover up your fears or get back at people out of frustration because you are unwilling to accept the present circumstances.

Acceptance is one of the most critical keys for living a heart-led life, and then being able to learn lessons from the things that do happen. You accept and then try to look at the things that are happening around you and people that are coming into your life and try to understand why you have attracted these things into your life; why you have attracted these lessons. Try to be honest with yourself and try to look at your intentions behind the actions that you are choosing to take. If you notice your own energy and actions, you will start to see the patterning in your own life and you will find these opportunities to learn lessons from these experiences rather than just fighting against them or becoming frustrated or blaming others or yourself and refuse to see the ways in which you can learn from these influences and how they are being presented to you by the energetic patterning of influence in the universe. The more that you gain a deeper faith in the Universal Energetic patterning, the more you will start to see that you can make different choices and you can learn from experience, you will start to change some of these repeating cycles that you experience over and over again from past lives or from soul imprinting.

Awakening

You can start to look more deeply inside yourself and outside at the circumstance by allowing yourself to see what the circumstance represents in your life and then begin to see what you may want to take on as a lesson. If you are truly vigilant, aware, and willing to take new actions, you can begin to change your vibrational patterning and evolve your soul.

This often happens in the form of some kind of an awakening. Sitting down right now could be an awakening for you. You can begin to look at your life as patterns and make new choices. Often when your soul is truly ready to be awakened on a really deep level, something major will happen. Some kind of awakening will occur. Something will force you or jog you into an awakening. Maybe it will come in the form of something that seems like a disaster to you. You might not understand why it happened.

If you choose to become more aware of the things that are happening in your life as lessons, you can allow yourself to really see these things as opportunities rather than roadblocks. Maybe you need to sit in despair for a few days and feel blocked, but if you start to wrap your mind around everything being a lesson and an opportunity, you will start to see how you can shed old patterns and change. You are being given the gift of a lesson.

This jolt of awakening may come in the form of losing everything. Maybe you will have to start over from zero. This could seem like a disaster and may cause you a lot of emotional pain and angst, but your soul may be stirring for some kind of change. It is ready for a new light, a new awareness, and is ready to shed old patterns and find new ways of being and relating.

During this period in your life, you may find yourself called to new interests, new awareness, new thought patterns, new lines of work, and new ways of spending your time. Some of these may be interests you have always had stirring deep within you, but you didn't take them seriously. Maybe you didn't think they were socially acceptable or something your family would be impressed by or something that would ever make you any money, but these interests are your soul speaking to you. Take them seriously. You never know what could come about in your life. They may come in the form of some kind of a nagging or deep yearning, and they may feel completely out of the blue or completely random. They may have been with you for a very long time, and they are important.

Listening to Your Soul

Soul evolution comes in the form of change, and it will deeply affect what you believe and how you pursue your true intention in life in faith and with integrity. These things may be strange or scary, but it's your choice to follow your soul's calling with faith and trust. You can just sit in your same old patterns, but that will manifest as disease or some kind of abusive situation or stagnant structure in your life. This is a gift. There is a reason why you are here right now, and there is a reason why you are listening.

There are changes that you could be making every moment of every day. New inspiration and new opportunities are always popping up. They are not always roadblocks. I am not suggesting that you follow every whim or follow the kite as it leads you. You can combine these longings with grounded spiritual guidance. If you have these deep longings, you may want to sit with a guide you really trust or sit in meditation so that you are clear that these are divine soul messages coming through and not just whimsical ways to get away from your deeper feelings. You will be able to understand your inner truth more deeply if you submit to following these kind of soul longings.

The ego can stop people from listening to deeper longings and yearnings and understanding if they are deeper yearnings or habitual ways of distracting yourself from your truth. Ego is a gift in a cerebral state of human form and gives us drive. The ego gives us a sense of well-being, of wholeness, and it gives us a reason to be here. The ego can get the best of us and take us away from our soul intention and into the same patterns of pain.

The Seven Deadly Sins

The seven deadly sins are pride, envy, gluttony, lust, anger, greed, and sloth. The seven deadly sins are presented in Catholic form as condemnation, but I am talking about them as transgressions in character that are fatal to spiritual progress. We all suffer from the same basic fears: loneliness, loss of faith, not understanding why we are here. We often feel hopeless and sometimes feel anxiety due to these questions. Why is my soul placed here in the material world? Why do I feel these longings? Why do I feel so out of balance and out of touch?

The mind functions as a tool to help us gain a better understanding of balance and the coexistence of human flesh in the spirit, the soul form we all partake in. When we are faced with deeper attacks on our core sense of self, we often turn to defensive attitudes of ego to survive. By remaining vigilant and witnessing your actions and attentions, you can learn to notice when you are falling into the basic pitfalls of character and integrity.

If we make this a chosen path of truth in our lives rather than succumbing to our fears and acting out of one of these character defaults, we can remain in spiritual alignment with soul growth and evolve within the organic patterning within the universal life force flow. If we push against truth and cover up with actions or defaults of character, we end up repeating the patterns and often feel victimized by the circumstances of our own lives.

Look again. You might not be living in line with your truth, and the fears and actions are able to confine you to a sheltered life maintained by pride, ego, and vanity. Intentions can be self-serving through fear rather than thinking with a collective truth and collective consciousness. The universal life force wants us to work together in a balanced flow. If we deviate from this, we cause ourselves and others much suffering in the long run. Spiritual illness is far more fatal than physical illness. The beginning stage of "soul sickness" manifests as physical illness in our bodies. The more we can work to be honest with ourselves and in tune with our spiritual truth and our soul calling, the more we will be able to manifest a truly higher vibration with our lives and live in line with our soul essence.

The seven deadly sins are a path to identifying how we cover up our true essence due to fear. I am not speaking in condemnation of how you live or the morality of your life. I use these references to explain the ways you can divert your character out of integrity and into a quick fix for when you are feeling a deep fear or a sense of imbalance. I urge you to begin to notice these things in your life and know that you can always make different choices. The only thing stopping you may be your inability to be aware and a fear of the unknown.

Start to notice when you feel imbalance in your life. Maybe you aren't clear about your inner truth. Maybe you don't feel completely confident in the choices you are making, the words you are choosing, or the actions you are taking. You might turn to one of these character defaults to feel better in the present moment, but this is not something that is really nourishing for your soul. It is just a quick fix to make your ego feel better.

You might turn to pride quickly if you feel that you are in a situation where you don't have a firm grip on the facts and don't know how to respond from a sense of truth. Instead of being honest with yourself about that and realizing that you might need to slow down, be a little more patient, and do a little more research, you want to keep up with the rest of the people around you. How many times have you turned to pride? We all do it, these are not condemnations of anyone; these are things to watch out for.

You can choose to take these actions and live a pride-led life, but oftentimes a person who does that is very unhappy on a deep soul and spiritual level. You might turn to pride and act like you are better or smarter than other people if you don't know what you are talking about and don't want to slow down enough to admit it and get humble.

You might turn to envy and feel you are the victim instead of the aggressor. You don't know what the next right action might be for yourself, but you don't want to be humble enough to let down your guard, turn to your inner truth, do some more research before taking action, check in with somebody to find out what they meant by what they said, or just slow down and stop to think. You might become angry with people and try to get what they have rather than sitting down and being honest with yourself about what the right action for you is to take. You might turn to lust. You might cover up by becoming the sexiest person you can possibly be or get as many women or men as you can to fall in love with you because you want to cover up the fact that you don't know why you are here or what the point of it all is.

It would be better to be honest with your soul that you are having a little fear or a little anxiety than immediately turning to this action of covering up through lusting after people. Perhaps it's gluttony. Perhaps you are covering up these intrinsic human fears by consuming a lot of substances or buying a lot of things or by being greedy and trying to cover up by owning a lot so that you can show it to other people. Your ego may feel more at ease, but your soul is still hurting.

There is a big difference between ego gratification and soul calming. You can feel it. You can look within to find out what makes you revert to a quick ego fix rather than having the patience and belief to follow what you know your inner truth is. Often, we each have certain aspects of life or circumstances that scare us or remind us of painful past experiences, and our way to resolve it is to revert quickly to an ego fix. These are powerful things to know about yourself. Only then will you be able to slow down, breathe, check in with what you are feeling, seek to learn what you truly need or want, begin to have patience and belief in the synchronistic flow of life, and make choices more aligned with your soul intentions.

Your soul is calling for a deeper experience, so if you make quick choices to feel better now—but have a nagging sensation that something is not aligned—you will close your heart, stress your body and mind, and become more attuned to illness and neurosis. Try to be vigilant about those things. Don't be hard on yourself, but just notice when you are turning to those things because true happiness and true serenity is in living a truth-led life. Oftentimes, your perception of what is real and what is valid is what is actually true.

You Are Divine

In your soul-consciousness, you are divine. You are a god or goddess experiencing "here." Your reality is just as valid as anyone else's. You are not meant to bend yourself around what you are told truth is or what society tells you that you are supposed to become because oftentimes, if you do try to do that, you will fall into one of the seven deadly sins. You will succumb to greed or sloth or envy and start taking actions that are coming out of aggression or passivity. You will also follow those paths when you think someone else's reality is better than your own. Your reality is the most valid, and your truth is the most valid for you to understand, accept, and communicate from this space.

Some people get a great joy from categorizing guides, planes, and perceptions. You might enjoy putting these things into categories be-cause it feels safer. You might have developed a beautiful method of describing the universe in logical terms and mental setups that assist you in perceiving and non-perceiving.

Many people have books that underline and outline the very structures of the universe as a complete ball of wax and a nice di-agram. There are many colors and levels and hierarchies of being. Dimensions and vibrations are all lined up in a neat package. If you are comfortable with the words, you can hold up your book and say, "This is how it is."

Not long afterward, someone or something comes along and shakes that conviction. You wonder, *Who is right?*

Some of you may cling to your comfortable truth by resorting to pride or ego. When your habitual faith is challenged and shaken enough times, you may open to finding a truth within you. This awak-ening is a new time for the soul to evolve. You sometimes need to drop old methods, diagrams, hierarchies, and neat packages. You sometimes have to go to that scary place, which is your truth and your own sanctuary of knowledge. You can choose to cover up with one of those ego-driven actions of pride or envy or sloth or jealousy or greed or money derivatives or sex derivatives to cover up your fears. You need to go to that scary place to find deeper knowledge.

Contemplating Truth

There is no greater truth than the one that percolates within you. All stories are meant to be changed. All concepts are meant to evolve. All ideas are meant to expand. That is why every conception of the be-ginning of being is in essence true to the degree in which it rings true to the heart of the individual. Every level of truth is not less than the greatest or highest truth, but in reality, it is a reflection of that truth. It only becomes dangerous when we try to force our truth onto other people. That is usually coming from a sense of invalidity or inferiority. If we do not know what we are doing in the world or why we are here, we may try to force our truth onto other people to make them believe it. That is resorting to one of the seven deadly sins rather than living from a true place of honesty, integrity, and grace—in your own sense of truth.

To my understanding, Einstein's theory of relativity pointed out that events are perceived at different angles, levels, or perspectives. The truth of that event is relative to the perceiver. Three observations of the same event may be completely different, but all are true because each observer is perceiving according to their own perspective. This works the same way on every level of perception. Truth is enormous. Truth is owned by the perceiver. It is impossible for anyone else to know what is true for you, for yourself, for your soul, except for you.

Every observation you make is a reflection of your own truth. Every perception you have is a reflection of your inner truth. Every bit of data you collect and every bit of information you gather is constantly reflecting the content of your own truth. Your life circumstances constantly mirror your own truth. If you want to know what your truth is, observe your existence. Observe the data you collect, observe your information about others, and observe the things that are said to you about others. Those things reflect your truth for you. Those things reflect exactly what you believe. As truth is multifaceted, and it is flexible, dynamic, and always willing to change.

Your truth can change. Your belief system can adjust to alter or transform chaos in your life. In understanding the profound relativity of truth, from your own perspective, it follows naturally that one would begin to understand the validity of someone else's truth and see the world from someone else's point of view. Truth on your plane is forever evolving, mixing, churning, and becoming more of what it was a moment before.

The only thing that is not an illusion is love. All things are variations of this energy moving through creation. From love, all consciousness is seeking that highest truth. We are all on all planes, evolving toward that greatest of truth, and no matter which path you choose, it will eventually lead to god or goddess or universal life force incarnate in energetic form.

Choose your path to creation. Choose your path and return to that universal life force light. Realize that perception is relative and the reason that truth remains constant in your reality is that your internalized mass consciousness deems it so. Moving down from the mass consciousness to continents, nations, cities, groups and, finally, individual truth, becomes intimate, personalized. That is where truths collide, change, and combine. You are learning to integrate your truth and accept the validity of others' perceptions. You have gone the route of acknowledging your truth. No more killing one another in disputes over truth but instead acknowledging your own truth, living in the truth, and acknowledging the validity of other people's truth and perceptions. Now is your time for growth and evolution in ideas and perceptions. Start asking questions and speaking aloud about what is happening in your life.

Yearning for Change

You may be experiencing deep soul yearnings. You might be experiencing a deep yearning for adventure or discovery. You might feel a yearning to explore a new belief or discover a distant land. You might not know why. If you do go ahead and explore it, it could reveal a deep desire, a deeper yearning for your soul, or a deeper calling. You could very well expand your horizons beyond your wildest dreams.

If you are able to set aside your usual activities and engage in new explorations, you may wish to consider taking a day trip or planning a longer excursion in the near future. You can also expand your horizons in emotional and spiritual ways today or any other day by opening your mind to exploring new ideas and belief systems. A good way to begin this process is to sit quietly in meditation and imagine your awareness reaching out. Imagine your awareness expanding far and wide into the world around you. Attuning to the rhythms of life and putting forth energy will attract many new opportunities for growth. Every aspect of your life seems magical and sacred when you open your mind and expand your awareness to the world around you. You often become so accustomed to your usual routines that you fail to notice the opportunity for discovery and learning, the lessons in every moment. Simply by choosing to heighten your awareness of the world around you, other people's perceptions, and your own truth, you may feel inspired to discover and explore newness. You might feel inspired to open your mind to these new possibilities. You might feel inspired to transform your old expressions into new ones.

Mindfulness
Journaling Practice 8

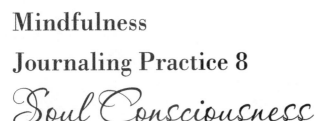

Soul Consciousness

Some simple questions can help you become more attuned to the deeper desires in your soul consciousness. Sit with them every few months or so. These changes happen gradually, but they need to be looked into consistently over long periods of time.

Are there things you feel especially attuned to? Are there people you don't always feel you resonate with? Are there people you feel you have a deep understanding with? Why is my soul placed here in the material world? What do I long for? When do I feel out of balance, out of touch? When I am most afraid? What aspects of the seven deadly sins do I turn to most? What am I really seeking? What do I dream about achieving? Do I know why? Where am I stuck in repetitions? What do I keep seeing or hearing as messages in my life? Am I consistently conflicting with the same person? What can I learn from this? What stops me from looking more deeply within myself? What am I getting out of staying in the repetition? What am I afraid will happen if it changes? What can these repetitions in my life teach me? What are the similar patterns within each? Can I accept the repetitions and continue to learn from them? Can I avoid falling into passivity? Can I find active acceptance and observance while I navigate my soul consciousness and transformation through these experiences?

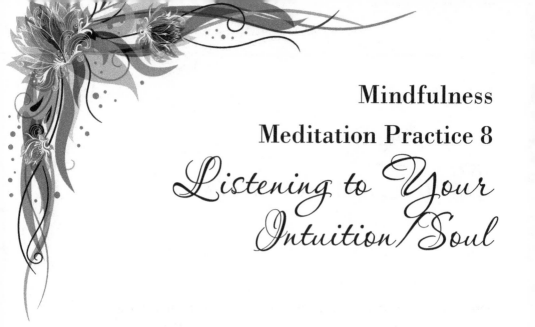

Mindfulness
Meditation Practice 8
Listening to Your Intuition/Soul

Simply sit or lie down. See where you are with finding your breath and connecting to your body energy. Has this practice become easier and more accessible to your everyday way of life? See where you are holding tension and imagine life force flowing into those areas of your body and mind. Simply listen within. Listen to the thoughts that pass. Listen to your heartbeat. Listen to the intuitive or soul-led voices within you. Begin to hear and fear-based voices. Open your mind to an even bigger space, limitless expansion of expanded awareness. Listen to the voices or messages that come through there. Try to feel it in your body. What is your truth? What are your fears? What are your projections? Take the time to find the soul-led and heart-inspired voice within. This is your intuitive voice. Cultivate a relationship with stillness. Tune into this internal truth as often as possible. You might not understand what or why you are feeling and experiencing these thoughts and feelings. Simply listen and learn to trust your intuitive or soul-led guidance.

Chapter 9

Chakra Cleansing and Balancing Your Body's Energy

In this chapter, we will discuss the practical definitions of the age-old mysterious concept of chakras or subtle energy in your body. I will teach you what each chakra means and how to listen to your body to identify where you are holding emotional and physical blocks. The practice of cleansing and balancing chakras promotes letting go of traumatic body memory and developing total awareness through learning to balance body energy. At the close of this chapter, journaling and meditation practices will help you understand how to cleanse and balance your chakras as a daily practice toward healing and total enlightenment.

Chakra is a Sanskrit word that means "wheel of spinning energy." The Taoist term for these energy centers is "don tien." When we refer to chakras, we are speaking about the subtle energy bodies and not the physical energy body. They have been described as energy organs—as the kidneys and heart are physical organs—that are vital to human health. The energy they draw is metabolized and distributed throughout the body, down to the cellular level.

There are seven major chakra centers in the subtle energy body. They are energetic representations of the energy fields created by the body's endocrine glands.

B. K. S. Iyengar, an Indian teacher of hatha yoga, says, "As antennae pick up radio waves and transform them into sound through receiving sets, chakras pick up cosmic vibrations and distributes them throughout the body."

Energy flows into your chakras from the world around you, out to the world from within, and up and down between them. There are also other subtle energy centers in your knees, feet, and hands—along the meridian lines—but these are the seven main chakras:

✵ Mula Darha chakra (root chakra)
✵ Shashistahna chakra (pelvic center chakra)
✵ Mana Pura chakra (solar plexus chakra)
✵ Yanahata chakra (heart chakra)
✵ Visudu chakra (throat chakra)
✵ Ajna (third eye chakra)
✵ Sahasrara chakra (crown chakra)

The Meaning of Chakras

You don't have to "believe in the chakras" to be able to benefit from the awareness practices in these chapters. Some people need scientific proof and definition, but to my knowledge, no one has been able to measure these energetic centers. There are all kinds of discrepancies between healers and yogis as to what color each area is represented by. Each color is meant to express a different frequency created by certain energies or feelings. One of the oldest yogic texts, *Upanishads*, mentions seven chakras, their names, and their "bija sound" or corresponding vibrational pitch and sometimes a mantra. The chakras go up and down the seven-note scale in the key of C Major.

Ultimately, the proof of their existence doesn't matter so much because from what I have experienced and researched, they are useful in helping people describe and own their human needs and correlate them with physical sensation.

Almost everyone, even those who claim no faith in their origin, can feel the sensations related to the chakras. Experience often leads to faith, or suspended belief, and through your own sensations of these subtle energy fields in your body during these practices, you will undoubtedly learn to cultivate and channel deeper circulation throughout your visceral being. When your sexual energy moves through your being, it is modulated and transformed as it passes through each of these chakras, producing different sensations, feelings, sounds, and colors, which will melt blocks by promoting self/soul understanding and deeper balance, opening your mind to a timeless, placeless, trance-like existence.

You can circulate your life force energy more fluidly throughout your visceral and energetic being. I will provide a brief understanding of the chakras and describe some of their qualities. Reflect on your own experiences now. Listen to your body as you read. Chakra sensations can be felt when you are nervous or afraid about a decision you have made or a presentation you are giving to your peers.

Many people describe feeling a movement or tension in their stomach, which is where the third chakra is located. Your third chakra is associated with identity, your source of confidence, and your sense of self. You might feel tightness in your throat when you feel emotional and afraid to say what you feel. This is the area where your fifth chakra is located. It is your center for assertion and communication. Another area you may be able to recall feeling from time to time is in your second chakra. People often describe a warm melting sensation in their lower belly when they feel aroused or creatively or athletically "in the zone." Your second chakra is a source of (pro)creative energy.

Your fourth chakra, your heart, may be where you are most familiar with sensation responses. That is where love flows and heartbreak resides. The root chakra or first chakra is in your pelvic floor. It is associated with stability, security, and survival issues. You might feel tightness in that area, the lower back, or procreative organs when you are moving residences, having financial troubles, or undergoing professional scrutiny. Luckily, these physical symptoms are simply signs that your body is seeking attention and wants your mind to unify with its resonance.

You can use practices to help with total awareness for your mind-and-body union. Eventually, through experience and practice, you will understand the sensations in your body as they relate to all seven chakras. You will be able to harness this ability to cleanse and cultivate your life force energy for your own healing and transcendence. The more care and sensitivity you give to your body, the more balanced and open these centers are, the easier it will be to move and transform your energy.

Melting Chakra Blocks

When your chakras become blocked, you often feel physically or mentally sick and out of balance. You can melt these blockages through emotional understanding, deeper intimacy with self, and circulating your sexual energy to create more balance and stability in your being. Helping energy flow freely through your body assists you in becoming a whole, healthy, human being, allowing you to access your natural power and communicate in a fluid and graceful way.

Your life force energy flows from your grounding root and up through your sexual center and is transformed through your chakras. If you are holding blocks in these seven subtle energy fields, they are often related to life circumstances or outlook, which can become blocked. Because the energy also flows up and down your internal being, representing a path to discovering more about what aspects of your life are causing you conflict, you will discover where you are holding this blocked intra-psychic processing. Each chakra can give you information about what aspects within your personality, what areas of character, are seeking spiritual development.

Your chakra may be more closed on certain days than others and more open on other days. It is good to begin to notice when you are reacting to something in your life. Ask yourself if you are acting or feeling from a place of fear and notice what fear you are coming from. You can determine which chakra the fear is associated with and then sit down to do a meditation to open, cleanse, and balance the subtle energies in this chakra. You can open yourself up to experiencing all of your different feelings around the issue and patiently and with humility choose the actions you would like to take.

Remind yourself to look at the positive. Each chakra can give you information as to what aspects within your personality, what areas of character, are seeking spiritual development. By working with your chakras, you can also learn to direct your own personal healing and spiritual growth by identifying what is blocking you and why you are blocked. What am I experiencing today or currently in my life that would make me feel more open here or less open? How do I perceive life in a way that would make me feel less or more open here?

Balancing Chakra Energy

I welcome you to take my hand, hear my voice, and join my spirit as we discuss practices and meditations that help you attune and balance your chakras. These are much more physical and experiential that simply reading about them. Tune in to you.

Healing Trauma

If you have been through physical or emotional trauma, your chakras may be especially sensitive. If the trauma is too much for your brain to process, your body may keep you safe by hanging on to it until your mind can process it. This is why we see so many trauma victims with memory lapses and physical impairments. Your brain is defending against overstimulation and leaves much of the experience in the body. This is a survival mechanism. If memories arise from these chakra exercises,

- ❈ Seek therapy from a specialized practitioner.
- ❈ Take hot baths. Epsom salt can help cleanse the visceral tissue from toxins, and lavender helps relax the mind and body.
- ❈ Deep breathing and interoception (in a safe environment) will help you feel the sensations and open up pathways for the emotion to move through you.
- ❈ Talk with others whom you trust.
- ❈ Write in a journal.

❖ Talk to your inner child. Ask what organic and natural healing you need—and give it to yourself.

❖ Don't try to push yourself into total awareness too quickly. Healing is a lifelong process and should be respected as such. Take your time and peel the layers slowly.

❖ Love yourself and your defenses! They are there to protect you!

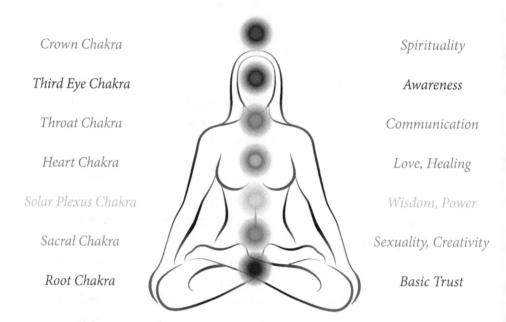

Crown Chakra — Spirituality

Third Eye Chakra — Awareness

Throat Chakra — Communication

Heart Chakra — Love, Healing

Solar Plexus Chakra — Wisdom, Power

Sacral Chakra — Sexuality, Creativity

Root Chakra — Basic Trust

Your Step-by-Step Chakra Lesson

Chakra One (Root Chakra)

This chakra is called the "Mula Darha chakra." The sound of this chakra is *lahm* (long A) in the musical note of C. The color of this chakra is red. The body parts associated with this chakra are the adrenals, the perineum, the anus, the blood, the lymphatic system, the teeth, and the skeletal system.

The first chakra is located at the root of your sexual center. It is at the coccyx, at the base, right near your perineum, which is the central spot on a man between the testicles and the anus. On a woman, it is the small space between her vagina and her anus. Try touching your root chakra and see if you feel sensation moving up into your genitals. Do you feel numbness, blockage, or even shame in touching yourself?

When your first chakra is open, you will feel very secure. It is the chakra that represents safety and security. Oftentimes, this safety or security is financial or emotional. For most people, those are the two things we need to feel safe enough to function in a balanced way. Ultimately, we need to feel connected to other living things. When your first chakra is open, you will feel this security and calm, you will feel motivated, you will welcome change, and you will adapt well to new circumstances. Your adrenal glands will regulate your fight-or-flight reaction that usually responds to threat and danger with the release of two hormones: adrenaline and nor-adrenaline or epinephrine and norepinephrine. The adrenal glands determine how well you manage stress in your life. When your body manages stress well, you will experience deeper courage or calm in the face of threats and danger. You will be able to act out of confidence rather than out of fear. You will be able to carry out your own actions.

When your first chakra is blocked or closed, you will often feel insecure, paranoid, or threatened if change is happening in your life. You might want everything to remain the same. You might need everything to be exactly the same every day because you need a feeling of control. You might eat at the same café every morning, need everything to happen exactly at the same time as the day or week before, and not be very flexible when certain things need to change. If they do change, you may overcompensate by trying to make things—or yourself—perfect. You may be fanatical about orderliness or cleanliness. You may be incapacitated if something is dangerous or stressing you out. You may bully people who don't have as much as you have or who threaten you in some way. Rather than just being confident in yourself, you may need to belittle people who are not confident or pick on them. You might not reach out to help them, and you may hurt them.

You can touch your first chakra as a healing tool. All you have to do is put your finger on that area of your body. Lie on your side or sit up and reach one palm across your lower pelvis from the front and one across from the back, like you are cradling yourself. While you hold this position, you visualize the color red. Whatever shade you naturally see in your mind's eye is your individual taste, but it is usually recommended to use a deep shade of red.

Then make the sound *lahm*. You can make the vowel really long. Feel the vibration moving through you. Also, let some emotion out if it's there. All vowels represent emotion. If you have a recorder, a piano, or a master pitch pipe, this is great. You can place any red, black, brown, or silver stones or crystals between your hands and body while you do this in meditation. These stones carry a certain vibration and will help cleanse the vibrational force of your chakra in that area. Then visualize the energy in this root chakra spinning. Imagine this deep red smoke or fire or fog, something thick, spinning in a clockwise direction. It could be a propeller rotating, something swirling in a clockwise direction while visualizing red and singing, "Lahm." Imagine that your chakra is grounding into the earth and opening and allowing the energy there to be purified. The energy in your root often gets really backed up. This is helpful when you feel you have left your body—and your mind is anxious.

Second Chakra (Pelvic Center: Sexuality/Creativity)

This chakra is called the "Shashistahna chakra." The sound of your second chakra is "vahm," and its note is D. The color of this chakra is orange. Your organs most closely associated with this chakra are your kidneys, bladder, small intestine, large intestine, colon, rectum, and anal canal. It includes all reproductive organs.

Your second chakra is located at your belly, in the center space between your hips, about two finger widths below your navel. Those organs are really important to keep healthy because we hold all of our emotion there. The most common forms of cancer are in our reproductive and hormonal organs. We want to keep our cells as in tune vibrationally as possible. This happens through mind-and-body union.

Open

When your second chakra is open and vibrating, you will feel confident and balanced. You will trust that the universe will provide all that you need because you actually experience abundance by just being in your body. When you feel positive about your life, your ability to be abundant, and your own natural wonderfulness, you will attract more money and success because you will be asking more generously with yourself—and then more generously with others. You will naturally attract more abundance.

The more uptight you are about holding on to all of your possessions, pushing people away, or judging or worrying about the future, the more you are going to attract that kind of energy into your life. The laws of attraction are that positive attracts positive, negative attracts negative, and you really want to get in tune with feeling abundant naturally. You are as alive and as in tune and as open in your body as you allow yourself to be. The more open your second chakra is, the more open you will be with your own sensual body. Open yourself to your core. You will experience much greater passion.

Blocked

When your second chakra is blocked or closed, you may be stingy or protective of what you have out of fear that you will lose it and not be able to get more. You might be really materialistic. Not having enough money will be a constant worry so you are constantly thinking about not having enough. You might feel a lot of fear about yourself as a sexual being and may feel that you are not enough. Be aware of and start to work on yourself.

Open your hands, keep your fingers together, and extend your thumb at a right angle. Your index finger and your thumb form an L shape. Your left hand forms a reverse L-shape. Place your thumbs on your hips and move the longest fingers on each of your hands toward each other, resting your palms on your stomach, or it can be reversed, placing your hands on your lower back. When you are holding your hands in this position, it brings healing energy to your organs. You can begin to generate some massage in your stomach area. This is excellent for rejuvenating your kidneys, relieving lower back pain, opening up your intestinal area, letting your blood flow in that area, and allowing your breath to really open up into your sexual center in your second chakra.

Hold this position while you visualize the color orange and make the vahm sound. You sing D. Place orange crystals, flowers, or cloth between your hands and skin while you do this meditation. Visualize the energy in your chakra spinning. Try visualizing smoke or fog spinning or swirling in a clockwise direction. Visualize the energy in your second chakra spinning in a nice clockwise motion, allowing the vibrations in your second chakra to really open. Imagine that you have a truly healthy, flowing second chakra.

Opening the first and second chakras together is a very nice daily practice. Open those two together. Most of us hold a lot of tension in our first and second chakras because we just have to get by every day. We have so much to do and end up feeling overwhelmed or don't take time to process all that we take in from the outside world and all we experience internally. There are often many things that we think that we are consumed by when we can also put our attention into our bodies, opening up our energy centers, and connecting to the earth and others this way.

The more deeply you connect with your own body, the deeper your experience of pleasure and abundance can be. Your natural energy force and subtle energies are getting freed up. We are gifted so much with these bodies and energy centers in our bodies that connect to universal life force. When we breathe deeply, the breath turns into energy. We spend so much time being separated from our bodies through judgment, critical thinking, and visual stimulation that we end up constantly igniting the nervous system through visuals or the way we look at people, judge them, and separate ourselves from them. We end up separating from our own bodies.

Third Chakra (Solar Plexus/Center:
Identity and Confidence)

This chakra is called the "Mana Pura chakra." The sound of this chakra is *rahm* (long A) in the note of E. The color of this chakra is yellow. The body parts associated with this chakra are your stomach, pancreas, spleen, gallbladder, liver, muscular system, and skin. Your third chakra represents your will.

Open

Your third chakra is located at your solar plexus, between the belly button and breastplate (not as high as the breast). When you are balanced, you will feel balanced. You will be able to experience everything, both positive and negative emotions, but you won't be consumed by them. Feelings will be more able to simply flow through you. You will be self-motivated and able to express your will in a way that is free of ego. You will be able to express getting what you want without placing anyone else at a disadvantage—or manipulating anybody or yourself.

You will be a good decision maker and leader, emanating confident charisma that will lead others to select you for leadership positions, and you will be able to fulfill those positions in a confident, charismatic, and laid-back way. You will also be able to be more tolerant of those who have different viewpoints, lifestyles, values, and appearances because you will be confident in your own self and your own path. Staying on your own path is the most important thing in life. Staying on your own path rather than focusing on comparing or judging others is a sign that you are aligned with your own confidence and path.

Blocked

If you notice that you are falling into comparing and judging, opening your third chakra can rebalance your sense of self, will, purpose, and confidence. Another sign that your third chakra is closed is how you view your body. You may think you are too short, too fat, too whatever—and this may have nothing to do with objective reality. You may be enthusiastic one minute and depressed the next. You may become consumed by power struggles that cause you to feel undervalued or make decisions out of a fear that you won't get what you think you deserve. You might lack motivation and experience troubles with your liver, bowels, spleen, or stomach. This is due to worrying so much.

It is a wonderful thing to make a daily practice of checking in with your third chakra. We spend a lot of time in action and trying to create things in our lives, and this can cause problems with our third chakra.

Gently thump your palm against your solar plexus for about fifteen repetitions and then rub your open palm against your solar plexus in a clockwise direction over your solar plexus for about a minute. You can also do this for your child, a lover, or an elderly person. While rubbing your palm clockwise, visualize the color yellow. Make the sound rahm and sing it on a vowel. Your third chakra represents your will. Many people like to chant in Sanskrit "Sat Nam" or "I am" when opening this chakra. You can use yellow crystals or cloth while you are doing this meditation. Visualize the energy in your chakra spinning— yellow smoke, fog, or a propeller—in a clockwise rotation. Imagine yourself in the world, confident and seen. You are not hiding or ashamed to be seen.

Fourth Chakra (Heart: Emotion/Love)

This chakra is called the "Yanahata chakra." The sound of this chakra is *yahm* in the note of F. The color of this chakra is green. The body parts associated with this chakra are the heart, lungs, thymus glands, and cardiovascular system. Your fourth chakra is located at the center of your breastplate, above your thymus, and primarily in your heart center, between your nipples and armpit.

Open

When your fourth chakra is open, you will freely give and receive both romantic and unconditional love. You will be able to forgive hurts and extend much more compassion to people by trying to understand where they are coming from rather than judging. You will be more trustworthy and reliable, and you will have a deeper capacity for commitment. You will be more richly aware of the present moment by being able to drop into your senses more. You will be in touch with your feelings—both positive and negative—and your relationships will be of higher priority for you. You will have a strong connection to your family and your community. You will find happiness despite the circumstances in your life because you will have a grounded sense of belonging on this earth and accept the natural flow of your life. You will be able to laugh frequently and share your joy with others and with yourself. You will experience relationships and moments of sexual ecstasy with your partner because you will be that open. You will look at your life with more focus on gratitude for what you have and the beauty that is within and around you.

Blocked

Your thymus gland is aligned with your immune system function. If you keep your heart chakra open and become ill, you will be able to heal more quickly than if your chakra is closed. If closed, you will also have great difficulty communicating in relationships. You may shut down your feelings, become dull and predictable, feel alone a lot, move from one relationship to another, use thinking, reason, and intellect for your refuge, become a workaholic, work constantly to get away from experiencing people, and look at your life as half empty rather than half full. You might find that you grieve for months or years over something or heal slowly.

Stimulating and Opening

Follow the heart meditation and add the following:

Take a set of colored pencils. Draw a picture of how your heart feels when it is closed, protected, and shielded. Draw your heart however you imagine that it is closed, however it comes out of you. Be a child and draw what comes to you and then lie down on your back with your chest bare. Take some rose essential oil and put it on your left finger-tips and rub that into your heart chakra in a nice clockwise direction. Continue in a clockwise direction, imagining the color green. Put a nice piece of green silk, green stone, or rose petals with green silk over your heart chakra and continue to rub in a clockwise circle.

Put your left palm over your heart chakra, cover your left palm with your right palm, and softly chant the sound yahm for four minutes. Repeat this exercise four days in a row. Wash the silk every day after you use it to soak up vibration—and wash your hands. It is like you are drawing the pain or the closure out of your heart. Only use the drawing the first and the fourth day. You will feel more alive, stimulated, closer to your inner child, able to express what "I am feeling," and involved with what you are passionate about" without holding back or feeling self-conscious. Your sexual center and your heart are closely connected. If the two are separated, you don't have much by way of grounding in your life that will allow you to be attuned to your passions and create the things you want in your life.

Fifth Chakra (Throat: Assertion/Expression)

This chakra is called the "Visudu chakra." The sound of this chakra is *hahm* (long A) in the note of G. The color of this chakra is blue. The body parts associated with this chakra are the throat, thyroid, and parathyroid. Your fifth chakra is located at the center of your throat, by your Adam's apple.

Open

When the fifth chakra is open, you will find your own voice more easily. You will be able to express yourself more easily and clearly—both verbally and nonverbally. You will have more fun whistling, singing, listening to music, or writing music. You may be more of a quick thinker and a more articulate speaker. You might be excited by ideas and take pleasure in having deep conversations with other people. Your thyroid gland acts as your body's accelerator pedal. It speeds up your metabolic rate and the rate of chemical reactions inside your cells. This influences your energy level. When your fifth chakra is open and your thyroid is healthy, you will easily maintain your ideal weight without having to carefully monitor what you eat. You will generally feel full of energy and motivation.

Blocked

When your fifth chakra is blocked or closed, you may find it difficult to express your ideas and opinions. Speaking in front of people will make you nervous, and writing will be difficult for you. You will probably avoid taking a firm stand on controversial subjects. This is your voice. Opening the fifth chakra can bring you confidence about what you want to say.

This meditation is centered around chanting—alone or with a partner. Work your voice up and down the octave scale on the sound hahm. Close your eyes and visualize blue swirling in a clockwise rotation at your throat as you chant. If you are with your partner, you can bring your chanting into harmony with one another. It is a really nice extra vibrational force in your body, and tuning in together is a wonderful experience. You can do this every day. Additionally, you can chant until words, like a stream of consciousness, come through you. Something you have been trying to say or verbalize from within or something you wish to manifest may come to light through connecting root, to sex, to I am, to heart, and then to vibrational existence in assertion through voice.

Sixth Chakra (Third Eye: Intuition)

This chakra is called the "Ajna." The sound of this chakra is "Aum" long O in the note of A. The color of this chakra is indigo or deep blue. The body parts associated with this chakra are the pituitary or master gland and pineal gland (this is also discussed in the section for the seventh chakra). Your sixth chakra is located at your third eye, between your eyebrows. This is also a pressure point in reflexology, and when you touch it, you will feel a spongy layer there, which is perfect for your index finger to rub.

Open

When your sixth chakra is open and vibrating, you will quickly see and understand what is actually going on in any circumstance. You will be have insight and know what to do or not to do in almost any situation. You will exhibit wisdom, a quality beyond intellect, knowledge, or experience. You will have an innate ability to see the core of things. You will have vision. You will have the ability to imagine how the future could be and gain an influence over how the future actually turns out without reverting to being a controlling person. You will have more confidence in staying on your path and making choices that are evolving from a deeply intuitive place within you. Some people who have very open sixth chakras can have ESP (extrasensory perception) that allows them to see people's auras or future-oriented things.

Your pituitary gland regulates your growth hormone and your sex hormones: estrogen, progesterone, prolactin, oxytocin, and testosterone. If this chakra is open, you will find that you may age more gracefully—and you may be able to experience deeper states of rest and longer exercise periods.

Blocked

When your sixth chakra is blocked or closed, you may place a very large importance on education, acquired knowledge, and experience.

While those things are important, we don't want to devalue or forget about relying on natural wisdom and intuition. Needing to acquire knowledge to prove intelligence is often a sign that the sixth chakra is blocked and that a person is really seeking self-reliance by listening to internal wisdom. Opening the sixth chakra can facilitate this. You will rely on your willpower to get what you want instead of trusting that things are working in their own universal law, and you will be reluctant to rely on others and want to do everything for yourself. You might have a strong sense that only you can do it well enough or right, and nobody else can. You might experience a sharp reaction to the idea that a larger force of energy is out there (some call it God). You might also feel victimized often. You will feel you need to remain busy all the time, and if you are not busy, you are not proving that you are worthwhile. You might have a tendency to be hyperactive or move rapidly. You may get bored easily, have little interest in sex, or use it as a diversion rather than a connection. You may have trouble sleeping and find that your sleep is easily interfered with.

Chanting "aum," lightly massage your third eye with first two fingers of either hand. Visualize the color purple spiraling out from your third eye and then penetrating deeply between your eyes, into your third eye and frontal cortex, all the way back into your medulla oblongata and the top of your spinal cord. Rotate your fingers nine times counterclockwise and then nine times clockwise. Listen to your chants and the messages or intuitions that come to you. Where do you feel unrest in your life? What you are avoiding hearing?

This practice is best done often since the third eye often becomes cloudy through the use of phone, computers, or busy lifestyles. Try to do this simple sixth chakra meditation at least three times a day. Some even like to do it six or nine times. Make it multiples of three—however many times you do it.

If you feel like you are overstimulated in this chakra, and buzzing to the point that you feel high or manic, lower the amount of times you do this and focus on grounding into your root, bringing the chakra flow into balance from the earth, especially through your third chakra center.

Seventh Chakra (Crown: Open Mind/ Universal Consciousness)

This chakra is called the "Sahasrara chakra." The sound of your second chakra is "ah." Its note is B. The color of your chakra there is white or lavender. Your body organs most closely associated with this chakra are your central nervous system, pineal gland, brain, spinal cord, peripheral nervous system, upper skull, and cerebral cortex. The sensory neurons carry sensory input from receptors to your central nervous system. Motor neurons transmit motor output from the central nervous system to your muscles and glands. Your seventh chakra is located at the top of your head or crown.

Open

When your seventh chakra is open and vibrating, you will feel really whole. In Kundalini yoga, we talk about the serpent. The serpent is a metaphor for pure consciousness and life force energy, located at the base of your coccyx. Your Kundalini serpent will uncoil and release as you create openings for it to flow freely up from the earth and through your chakra system. You will feel attuned in your subtle energy flow throughout all seven of your chakras, out your crown to the heavens, and then back down again throughout your subtle energy bodies. This mystical rate of vibration is always happening within and around the entire universe.

When people talk about their Kundalini rising, this is what that is. You are able to get in touch with yourself and your subtle energy centers, and you can attune yourself. You will often feel confidence that your faith can't be shaken, and you will believe that you are in touch with universal life force and are able to move energy. You will be able to heal others and yourself. You will feel a huge amount of freedom. You will move beyond desiring material gain, ego gain, or the need to prove your existence and wanting. You will experience a sense of freedom and spiritual connection when your crown chakra is really open and all the other chakras are flowing in harmony.

Blocked

When your seventh chakra is closed, you will be caught in an endless cycle of life and death, fear of life and death, and ego fears that relate to the circumstances of your life. Rather than feeling trust in the synchronicities of the universe and seeking to learn from what is presented, you will feel you are a victim to the laws of Karma and perceive events with a victimized attitude. "This has to happen to me because I have to pay my dues. I cannot change anything in my life." You might long to return to some kind of spiritual feeling, but you don't know how to get there. You might feel you are trying to force things to happen and that you haven't learned to surrender to allowing things to happen in their own way. Intellectually, you may understand that the lower vibrations can't command the higher synchronistic vibrations and circumstances of life, but you still don't know how to live in that reality. You might ask, "Is this all there is? Is there more?"

When you start to open your seventh chakra, try to work on the other six. Try to stay around nature as much as possible. Even in colder months, try to be in awe of the natural flow of seasonal shifts and weather phenomenon. In colder months, you can take walks in virgin snowfall, find glory in the lightness shining upon the bare branches of trees, and enjoy the stark sky and winter moons. Even opening the window and enjoying the brisk, cool air for short moments is showing appreciation for your life force's connection to the natural world's shifts, gifts, and moods. In warmer months, you will benefit from going outside, feeling the heat on your body, and allowing the light to permeate your cells. As your cells absorb heat and light, they begin to awaken and naturally become more alive.

Mindfulness
Journaling Practice 9
Chakra Cleansing/ Emotional

Journal on each of these sections. What thoughts come to you about your own life? I like this verbal exercise for expressing pent-up feeling. These are good ways to open your heart and chakras. Emotional expression can be done by speaking gibberish. You are not trying to make sense or need be concerned with how you are received. You are simply releasing whatever comes out of you. It can be primitive sounds, grunts to express feelings, or made-up language. This process relieves you from having to come up with words connected to emotions. It lets you express feeling and intention. The aim is to release whatever you are feeling. Try it! Don't be shy! No one is watching but you—and your inner child! Let the child in you speak!

Another fun way to release it is to allow yourself, like a child, to just have a small tantrum. It can look like laughing out loud, kicking the bed, or moaning, screaming, or crying. Just let out your feelings and excess energy. This exercise helps you express energy, frustration, resentments, or anger you may be feeling toward another or yourself. Act it out. Play! The aim is not to pressure yourself into feeling or perceiving in a certain way. Try to release and don't let negative energy, free-floating anxiety, or aggression rule you. Let it move through you.

We are humans, and we are all energy. You want
to move the energies in your body! You will feel lighter.
In this clarity and lightness, new awareness and perceptions
can enter your mind and body. You may even hear your reactions
and hidden feelings. You might ask your soul consciousness what
you are seeking to transform and manifest? Clear these blocks to find
intimacy with your truth.

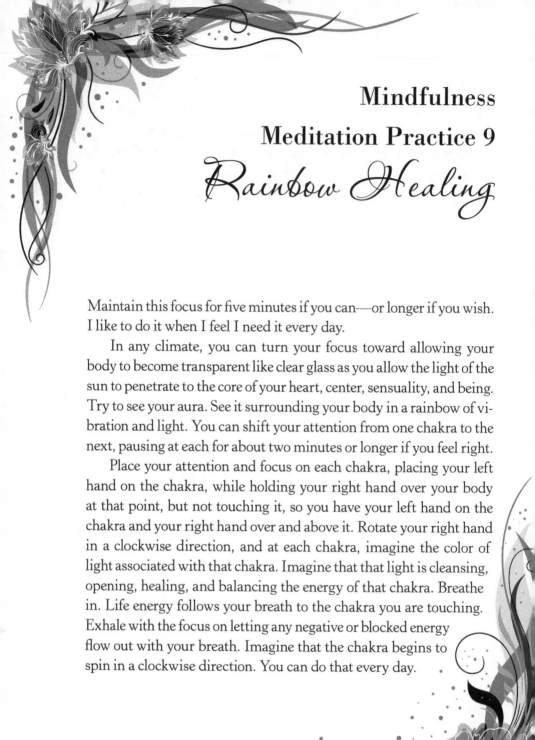

Mindfulness
Meditation Practice 9
Rainbow Healing

Maintain this focus for five minutes if you can—or longer if you wish. I like to do it when I feel I need it every day.

In any climate, you can turn your focus toward allowing your body to become transparent like clear glass as you allow the light of the sun to penetrate to the core of your heart, center, sensuality, and being. Try to see your aura. See it surrounding your body in a rainbow of vibration and light. You can shift your attention from one chakra to the next, pausing at each for about two minutes or longer if you feel right.

Place your attention and focus on each chakra, placing your left hand on the chakra, while holding your right hand over your body at that point, but not touching it, so you have your left hand on the chakra and your right hand over and above it. Rotate your right hand in a clockwise direction, and at each chakra, imagine the color of light associated with that chakra. Imagine that that light is cleansing, opening, healing, and balancing the energy of that chakra. Breathe in. Life energy follows your breath to the chakra you are touching. Exhale with the focus on letting any negative or blocked energy flow out with your breath. Imagine that the chakra begins to spin in a clockwise direction. You can do that every day.

Chapter 10

Fantasy and Daydreams

In this chapter, we will discuss how your fantasies and daydreams act as a vehicle for your mind. I will explain fantasy and daydream, where they originate in your mind, and how you can learn to observe your fantasies and daydreams as vehicles for understanding your deeper desires and intuitions. Learning to work through repression is a difficult journey for people who suffer trauma, and I take you on this journey with care and compassion because it is a helpful tool for letting go of repressed memory and fantasy and allowing yourself to become more deeply attuned to your spontaneous flow of vital life in the present moment. At the close of this chapter, journaling and meditation practices will help you listen to your fantasies, daydreams, and stream of consciousness as tools for letting go of stuck energy and developing a deeper connection with your intuitive voice and soul-led desires.

Fantasy

Fantasy is something that happens in the formless part of the soul, psyche, connection. A part of the soul or psyche needs to express primitive instinct but is aware—through relation and awareness of others in the material world of form—that we cannot carry out these fantasies. Fantasies serve as a healthy way to express desires and longings—without consequences.

In 1911's *Formulations on the Two Principles of Mental Functioning,*

Freud wrote, "Phantasy is a wish-fulfilling activity that can arise when an instinctual wish is frustrated."

Is your most primitive wish to be fused to your mother again in womblike resonance and symbiotic bliss? Is it to be fused with source energy or vibrational synchronicity? Most of the people in my practice have agreed that the womb represents the source. The womb is not a replacement for source, but it is the visceral experience we have all shared—and that we can most closely identify with what we imagine being unconditionally and completely held by source would feel like.

Fantasies, Daydreams, and Night Dreams

If most fantasies come to light to communicate primitive wishes that often have to do with human circumstance, emotional response, and desires by showing us psychical images, we may become curious about what our fantasies are showing us about ourselves. We can become curious about the stories and feelings by listening to our daydreams, night dreams, and fantasies. We can explore the psychic symbols that these fantasies form through the images our minds depict and identify emerging patterns by asking ourselves to observe and learn about ourselves. The conscious mind can develop more awareness and consciousness of how the soul's authentic essence and listening to inner desires can lead us toward greater fulfillment on this material plane.

The Origins of Fantasy

Have these images been unconscious all the time? Were they formed in the elusive unconscious? Where does the unconscious form? Are unconscious fantasies conscious fantasies, daydreams, or implicit memories that have been repressed?

The question of the exact birthplace of unconscious fantasy remains unanswered. Sigmund Freud concluded, "Unconscious fantasy is 'ambiguous and unclear; the vanished mental life of children. The forbidden wish which at some point appears in dream or piece of art.'"

I would suggest that the fantasies originate in visceral sensation of the cellular body, but where does this originate? We do not know. Longings? DNA? Implicit memory? Neuroscience has suggested that they are implicit memories formed in infancy before hippocampus development in the brain is stored in the amygdala. There have also been suggestions that unconscious memories are traces or imprints of DNA memory that have formed in your visceral being and communicated to your mind.

Don't become consumed by understanding their biological origin; instead, look at the images, feelings, and stories that create the landscape of our fantasies. Look at how we relate to these ephemeral, symbolic, and mentalized stories. Do you shame yourself? Do you ask yourself to look away? Do you laugh at yourself? Do you get high and numb them? Do you become curious and allow yourself to experience them? Do you wish to live inside of them and never step back into the conscious world of form? What do your fantasies, daydreams, and night dreams mean to you? How do they affect you?

Unconscious and conscious fantasies generally depict images of sexuality, birth, intrauterine experiences, and primal scenes—like destruction and seduction. They usually involve a subject that has supposed intentions and a relationship in which the subject wishes to do things to or with the object. Fantasy, daydreams, and night dreams seem to be survival tools or a symbolic way to express desire or transform excess psychic energy.

The importance of understanding where unconscious fantasy stems from falls to second place—behind finding healthy ways to express them. The goal is to try to invite and even accept these primitive wishes into consciousness to be observed and examined.

We are born into this world as a conflicting mass of energetic events. We are pulsing body energy contained in material body form. The urge to fuse with the mother as the symbol of the source of all of life exists in conjunction with the human urge to repel the mother as a way to individuate. This conflict lives within us in us to some degree—in imperishable ambivalence until the day we pass on. The desire to both individuate and remain connected to the mother, or source, shapes our response to this internal pulsing and creates the fantasy. When we repress this conflict, we become stuck inward, often stopping our momentum from actively aligning with our desires to manifest. This conflict ultimately stems from a libidinal desire for pleasure.

Repression

Let's discuss the positive use of repression. Many people think we need to be completely unrepressed beings. This is simply not possible, and it isn't healthy. Repression is a necessary function of the mind's instinct to live.

Repression is born from a need to defend against unconscious processes becoming conscious, the act of repression makes unconscious fantasy possible in the first place. The mind has instinctually protected itself by using repression as a tool for handling specific details of our own past that may overwhelm us.

There is a problem with using repression and deception as a tool for surviving aspects of your own mind. It may serve as a quick-fix solution to mental pain and psychic conflict, but a long-term repression as the mind matures and experiences may cause mental and physical illness. Unwanted libidinal instincts and repressed memories cannot ever win. At some point, the hidden trauma must be remembered.

Illness, at its root, is a way to communicate a message of desire to the world. Illnesses and anxieties manifest themselves like dreams. This imagery is always affecting the body, the nervous system, and the mind in varying degrees.

Pressure

When you are hanging on to unacknowledged inner pressure or are exposed consistently to overwhelming outside environmental stress and have no means by which to sublimate and express this pressure energy, your mind and body will become impacted by anxiety, stress, and ultimately terror. This high level of anxiety occurs when a person begins to feel a loss of sense of self or a loss of sense of the other.

Most of us experience sensory enclosure naturally, daily, and take it for granted. Most people have existential questions—How did I here? What is the point? Am I valid?—but employ mental distraction to create internal conflict. These conflicts are acted out in behaviors such as shopping, dating, or looking for the right circumstance in life.

If we lose grounding and revert to deep, fear-based anxiety, we can take a moment, close our eyes, clear our minds, and say, "What is my experience?" Turn your attention to what is happening in the moment: "I am standing on the floor. I can feel my body expanding when I breath. I can feel my heart beating. My experience is within my skin."

Our sense of time and space, self and other, will be restored.

Trauma and Fantasy

Be easy with yourself. Allowing the unconscious to come forward can invite deeply traumatic images and memories. This often happens with people who are holding trauma. Remain aware if you go deeply into primitive imagery and become too anxious or stressed. It is hard to discern which feelings are important to express right then. They can remain repressed, safe from too much shock at once. Skill and intuition help us make these choices in the moment.

Even when working through psychic blocks brings up uncomfortable memories or wishes, the experience of revealing the unconscious to the conscious mind is freeing. Much is revealed as you become aware of your own defenses and value the ways your mind and body actively protect themselves from too much information at once. Don't push. Simply observe. Take time, breathe, and walk. Journaling, therapeutic talk with a trusted practitioner, or healing touch with a trauma specialist—or someone you trust—can be helpful in working through deep trauma.

Expressive Mode

What lurks in the unconscious is comprised of the energy that creates a necessary life drive. Eros is libidinal instinct residing in our yearning to continue to live and create beyond free will. Love can become a more prominent experience for a person who expresses what is in the mind. This is discovered as we increase the ability to be with the depths and honesty of humanity—even as ugly as it can appear at times. If you seek an orthodox approach to some correction of self, to become something moral or socially acceptable, you are only continuing to serve psychic repression and conflict due to fears of feeling your true nature.

Expression helps your unconscious energies become more integrated with conscious thoughts. Expression of that energy by way of symbols, verbalization, recovering lost memories and fantasies, and sharing them with another, gives overwhelming feelings or desires the opportunity to become more consciously seen and known. The aim is integration of the many facets of self or selves, allowing you to increase conscious awareness of your inner life. This allows for consciousness of your impact on the world. This pursuit of developing deeper acceptance and awareness of self allows us broader choice of action and a larger ability for manifestation of fulfilling work, love, and play.

It is important to find modes of expression for unconscious fantasy. Psychic integration is well served through verbalizing, journaling, creativity, and daydreaming. Talking out, recording, writing down, and analyzing our daytime and nighttime fantasies or dreams, or bearing witness to our own creative works of art and the art of others are all ways of connecting with unconscious thoughts. We can learn about ourselves by observing and pondering the repetitions and paradigms. This allows us to explore avenues to healthy recognition and expression of these internal, unconscious fantasies and memories. This solace directly relieves pressure on the libidinal flow and fuels circulation, energy, and drive.

Discharge through words. How do I consciously find ways to observe, accept, and express? Let's learn to invite and observe the fantasies and daydreams that do come to the surface. Guided fantasy and the writing down of your most memorable fantasies are helpful tools for learning more about the feelings you are harboring and the desires your soul consciousness is communicating. Give yourself trusting time, space, and opportunity for expression.

Honoring Fantasy

Let's learn to observe fantasy as an aspect of your subtle nature that seeks to communicate something to self and others. Many people keep their fantasies hidden from themselves and their partners. Often, they see their fantasies as shocking, overwhelming, voracious, shameful, or something to hide. Don't make yourself feel or say anything that is too distressing. This need to hold back is a communication in its own right. Everything is of value. However, when you feel consciously ready to discuss a fantasy, often a level of awareness and maturity increases, and deeper bonding with self and others ensues. Ultimately, we seek to express fantasies so that we can observe the patterns and desires they communicate. This expression is meant to pave the way to a deeper understanding of self—and not to shock or hurt others or ourselves.

Some men and women with active fantasy lives and introspective interests are quite familiar with the sorts of patterns that their minds tend toward. To others, opening the mind to free association can be new. Any form of symbolism or fantasy feels odd or new. This offers an opportunity for enrichening relaxation of the nervous system and opening the mind through somatic awareness. It is best done in stages. Awareness comes from discovering links between fantasies and emotional communications that deepen our understanding of internal desire and self.

While acting the fantasy out can be cathartic or fun and can transmute energy, the enactment is not always the most helpful way to understand and transform this wish energy. It can simply be going through the emotions while still employing your usual defenses. It is important to describe, appreciate, explore, and share fantasy. Here, you can listen within and understand what your inner self may be expressing.

Engaging in the use of fantasy as a tool for deeper self-understanding helps you become a person with more choice in action rather than being tethered to defending against fantasy or impulsively enacting the fantasy as a way to defend against deeper needs and feelings. This can be the source of sex addiction or a compulsive fetish.

Let's learn to use fantasy as a guide to explore the many rich layers of gold within your beautiful vibrant being. Let's help you find greater confidence by developing resonance with these human needs and longings calling from deep within.

Themes: Communications from Your Fantasy

Let's discuss some of the ways fantasies reveal arcs and themes that are personal to you. Try reflecting on how these ideas pertain to you. I will guide you through some simple fantasizing and journaling practices.

When an illustration of your mind manifests in detail, perhaps you begin to see a common theme. It's like a melody that the music always returns to when the song harmonizes, and the listener is left humming that particular piece. You may have recognized a symbol, unformed thought, memory, or scenario as your personal melodies, patterns, recurring visions. Let's explore what this recurring theme or pattern may mean to you.

Patterns and Enlightenment.

Patterns and fantasies shift and change throughout our lives. They change over time. These shifts in fantasies can be very elucidating for your introspective process. Fantasy and circumstantial patterns can be reflections of your most current repressions and deepest desires.

Different types of influences may paint the colors of your fantasies. In fantasy or daydreams, you may find yourself shying away from certain images and scenarios that begin to form and moving your mind back to something that seems more socially acceptable.

Intrapsychic scripts are influenced by cultural mores and are always expressions of the eccentricities of each person's mind. We have developed long-term ways of perceiving, desiring, and understanding the world and ourselves.

Inhibiting the free flow of your body-mind synching stops the fantasy from this quiet communication. Your false self, or persona, may be afraid to see this aspect of your true self in that moment. Having a fantasy doesn't mean you actually want the thing to happen or will go about making it happen. Fantasy is a private expression. Your false self has no idea what your soul consciousness or unconscious need to release. As you allow the initial concepts to flow through you, the images or scenarios could easily shift something else that is even more organic to your spirit.

Change is never a linear or long-term process. It is built on daily introspection, desire for self-awareness, and greater choice of action. This shift away from socially learned rules will happen as you give yourself freedom to follow the free associations and stories your fantasies present—with recognition and compassion for your personal ebbs and flows.

Fantasy as Discharge

A fantasy or daydream is simply a thought or feeling that arises in your mind in the form of symbols, wishes, and scenarios that are interesting to you for some reason. This could take the form of a special vacation, a certain kind of romance, your child succeeding at something they are struggling with, a sensual fantasy, or an image that invites excitement. Daydreams that come at fleeting moment in the day, unconscious primitive fantasies, are beyond our cognitive mental choice or control.

We all have sensual fantasies several times per day. Fantasy is some primitive longing, natural to human instinct. They don't make us dirty or shameful. If we acted on all of them, we would be predators, but we are using fantasy as a way to explore our internal landscape and express it. People who feel shame and repress fantasy are not self-aware, and they often become predators—acting them out "sideways" and hurting others and themselves.

Start to observe your fantasies and memories throughout the day. You will notice that certain images or scenarios return. Some may be sensual, in human contact, form, or natural settings like vacations or excursions. Your mind may continue to return to this moving image as a form of self-pleasure or discharge of energy. Often, you may hardly notice it. Your senses may or may not become aroused. Again, when consciously observing, you may judge yourself as boring, silly, shameful, weird, or embarrassing. Try to remember to remain curious about your inner life and not overly judgmental. Fantasies are just an image the mind conjures, and they are something, gifts perhaps, for you to experience and explore.

Fantasies are not meant to go straight from unconscious or even the conscious mind to action. You don't have to stop and become consumed. Simply notice. When we are able to become conscious and accepting of these fleeting fantasies and memories throughout the day, we will simply enjoy our fantasies and memories for what they are and what they can teach us about ourselves. Let your mind stretch out, in your own time, and as you feel safe to. Sometimes it's good to take a hot bath and let your mind wander. It's a lovely way to get in touch with your deepest wishes, just following your mind to wherever it takes you. Sometimes this reveals areas you want to do deeper for healing and emotional recovery, and sometimes it reveals areas you want to manifest more of in your life. Constructive fantasy is ultimately a form of self-soothing and self-awareness.

As you begin to take more interest in your inner movies, start to notice the images, feelings, desires, and objects. Perhaps you will see a common theme. Often your fantasies take the form of enactment. A repeated theme, communication, conversation, circumstance, or wish is like a recurring melody you are left humming after a particular piece. A daydream, image, or scenario can be your personal melody.

If you discover that you fantasize little or not at all, it's okay. You are not broken. I would suggest that you become mindful of paying attention to the moments in your day or night when something catches your interests. If you want to know where your unconscious fantasy is most attuned, try noticing what makes you look twice. It could a certain color, flower, fabric, the way someone treats you, the tone in a person's voice, or a style of dress. Perhaps it's an interaction between others, an image on a poster, or a dialogue exchange on television or in a film that piques your interest.

Many people who think they don't fantasize just don't pay attention to the thoughts within because they have been conditioned to remain consumed with tasking or accomplishing. This often happens when a person has experienced deep trauma, which creates anxiety in the mind and body. Perhaps you learned that allowing yourself to fantasize is a waste of time. "Just keep one foot in front of the other and work hard." Try to let go—in a constructive frame and a relaxed setting.

You can circulate positive energy by letting yourself become consumed by that which enlivens you. See if a perfume, a type of car, or a story in the paper leads you into a fantasy or free association. Give your brain space away from focusing on the completion of tasks. Let your mind float like a buoy on the top of the water. Don't worry—you will come back and complete everything.

Having fantasies, daydreams, and memories may seem to take a long time. If you look at the clock, you will see your concept of time shifting. A thirty-second mental movie can change the whole scope of your nervous system, mind, breath, and heart for the rest of the day.

Mindfulness Journaling
Practice 10
Fantasy, Daydream, and Memory

Writing down fantasies, daydreams, and memories your mind conjures is helpful. Do this practice daily. A few scenarios may help you understand this. Begin to observe the meanings of the images, emotions, and dramas playing out in your mind. Let your mind wander. Write what surfaces. Make it a more focused journaling as you become more attuned to your recurring moving images.

Let your mind wander. If you are feeling upset with someone, you might have a fantasy. It could be a fight where you tell them how you feel. It could be you conversing with them and working through it until you feel understood. Maybe you imagine seeing them and experiencing the emotions you feel at the time. It is just a fantasy.

The experience of the fantasy may be exactly what you need to allow the anger to work through you and experience some relief from holding in the anger. Releasing the pressure can shift your consciousness toward understanding what you need to do to let go of the poison of resentment.

Once you let go of the anger, you may find new forms of communication and perspectives. You may to see this person as a teacher in your life or someone you learn from through the mirror of their behavior. This can happen if you let the fantasy play out, fully feeling your feelings during the process, and observing later what the themes and wishes are communicating. Eventually, this fantasy will dissolve—and you will find a way to resolve the issue. If you defend it, it will get bigger and could lead to obsession or illness.

Another kind of fantasy may involve attraction. Perhaps you are attracted to someone. To pursue this in real life might only hurt others or yourself, yet the desire burns. Sitting down and letting yourself have a full-fledged fantasy about this person, then observing themes and feelings that revealed themselves in the fantasy, will allow you to experience more deeply what it is about them that you seek. Perhaps you will find that you are craving something of what they have, do, or represent in your life. This could lead to welcoming a new habit or interest in your life. Maybe you get more deeply attuned to a longing for a rejecting parent or a feeling you haven't processed yet. This person may represent something you are projecting onto them.

Through the expression of the fantasy, you can move past the fire of desire. Maybe you will begin to see that this person doesn't actually have these attributes at all. What you really desire is a discovery of these attributes in yourself. Here, fantasy is a helpful tool for you to begin to understand what you crave and need. The fantasy releases the pent-up desire and whatever else surrounds this wish. Eventually, this relief allows your mind and body space for new ideas, transformations, and wishes to come forth.

Maybe you begin to notice a theme in your fantasies that has to do with surrender or power. Maybe it's riches or total freedom from things and responsibilities. What does this say about where you are emotionally? What do you desire? What familiar relationship patterns are from your family of origin? Your unconscious is seeking that you become more attuned to these influences so that you can begin to be more conscious of your actions—and not just reactive to familiar and social emotional conditioning. Anything else come to mind? Write down the ideas.

Perhaps you are most consumed by fantasies of escape or survival. You find yourself wandering out into nature, serene and blissful by the sea, on top of a mountain overlooking beautiful landscape, fresh wind in your lungs, or out in the wild jungle, consumed by survival and natural animals. Are you tired of social culture? Do you want to be seen as strong and virile? Are you in a difficult relationship? Do these fantasies help you become free of frustration? These questions and answers can be interesting as you write them down.

Perhaps you are an onlooker in your daydream, watching other people enjoying some moment in time. Maybe you feel safe being untouched—but a part of the experience by watching. Perhaps you imagine yourself the star of your daydream? Someone who has achieved success and is admired gloriously by everyone involved, there to fill your every whim and desire? What does this mean to you? How does this relate to your past experiences and wishes?

Perhaps you often find yourself dreaming of being touched, caressed, held, or giving comfort and protection. How do you feel in either position? What does this mean to you? How does this relate to your past experiences and current desires?

I don't want to influence your fantasies, daydreams, or memories. Open up to exploring what is inside and think about how you might choose to look at them. Let the possibilities linger and wash over you. Reading these possibilities may help you open your subtle energy system and allow your mind to begin to flow freely from its own center.

The beauty of fantasies is that they are totally private. You might have a long-term partner you share everything with, and they will never know every aspect of your fantasy world. How can they know every part of you when you don't even know every part of your own self? The hidden aspects of the mind, the unconscious, are an elusive, winding and technicolor landscape of mystery, eroticism, hopes, dreams, sensuality, desires, fears, aggressions, and spirit. Why not explore the little that comes forth when it does?

Mindfulness Journaling Practice 10: "Stream of Consciousness"

Stream-of-consciousness journaling is a beautiful, personal tool. Writing down your free-form, free associative thoughts and images can offer an even deeper relationship with self. Stream-of-consciousness journaling helps you open your unconscious through this "streaming" pen-to-paper experience, and it helps you become more attuned to your intuitive guidance. Journaling is helpful because you can go back and read your passages as time progresses to gain reflective insight on your growth and your journey.

However, stream-of-consciousness journaling is really beneficial in uncovering deeper aspects of your feelings and longings. This kind of free association helps you access intuitive thought. This can help you find clarity in relationships, career, family, and spiritual matters. Artists often use this type of journaling to uncover blocks. Other people use what they put together over time for literary content, building a memoir, or writing fiction. Whatever your use, it's best not to try to write for any purpose at all. Just free-associate with no goal in mind and no judgment over content, text, grammar, or form. This is for you. Stream-of-consciousness journaling opens sensitive aspects of self that can be a vital aspect for life-affirming awareness and self-acceptance.

As we continue exploring this kind of journaling, guide yourself, move past your familiar, cerebral, linear state of mind, and sink into your somatic body. Sit down. Think back to the first few chapters of this book and see if you can guide yourself. Open your breath. Check in with acceptance of where you are now and what you are feeling. Use your somatic experience. Scan your body. Open your heart. Always go back to these steps when attuning your body, mind, and heart for opening. Hopefully you are using this technique throughout the day to check in with yourself and increase union throughout your mind and body.

Pick up your pen or open your keyboard. Engage at home, on public transport, or in a café. You can do this free and easy process anywhere. Try it daily for ten minutes or longer if you wish. Consistency is more important than length of time—as in most practices.

Let go of the conscious need to make sense and just move into writing. Let yourself write whatever comes to mind. Let out spontaneous thoughts, free associative imagery, and feelings. Write whatever you are feeling, experiencing, thinking, or wanting in this very moment. Don't think about spelling, punctuation, grammar, or language. Sit and write whatever you are feeling, experiencing, thinking, or longing for in this very moment. It can be a kind of fragmented, train of thought form of expression.

If a memory or fantasy pops up, let it flow. Don't stop to correct mistakes or rethink a sentence. Your writing can sound like anything, look like anything, or communicate anything. It doesn't need to be clear. As you continue writing, it will feel clearer and clearer. Don't get stuck on what someone reading it would think of you or what you think of yourself. Write. It is pure presence in the action of expression. I invite you to write. Just put pen to paper or fingers to keyboard and scrawl out whatever comes to mind. Find a free and easy flow from body to mind to body. This is not a performance or a goal-oriented exercise. Let your intuitive guidance move you, and when you are finished, you will know you are finished—for now.

Mindfulness Journaling
Practice 10: Themes of Fantasy

Here are a series of questions to help get you started. Look them over before, and again after, you write.

How do I feel right now?

What senses feel most alive in me right now? Do I find myself repeatedly returning to certain thoughts? Do I repeat certain wishes or longings? Do I find myself thinking that I need to gather more information to write? Am I able to just express the many different thoughts and feelings that flow through me? Am I trying to solve a problem or work out a communication with someone? What else comes to mind as I write? In what ways do I experience shame or negative thoughts? How do you I feel now in subtle ways? Is anything holding me in a web of negative thinking? What do I find pleasurable in the present moment? Do I find myself fantasizing? Can I allow myself to write freely? Do I feel or allow myself to express any romantic, playful emotions? What is the melody of this memory or fantasy? How is that personal to me?

This is where the psychoanalytic process of free association, enabling the unconscious to become conscious, intersects with mind-and-body practices. This is not a linear or rational process; it is rooted in a strong mind-body integration. The free access of memory, fantasy, and feeling is an integral aspect of this total integration.

Fantasy Journaling

As we progress in this kind of journaling, we begin to delve into and incorporate the practice of fantasy journaling. A fantasy journal is a notebook or computer file in which you write memories, fantasies, feelings, and impressions as they come to you. Fantasy journaling is a bit more focused that stream-of-consciousness journaling. We focus primarily first on memories.

When you notice a memory or fantasy in your mind, bring yourself into your body with breath, and take a moment to jot down whatever you were beginning to fantasize about. Even if you have a busy life, try to do it when you are able to. Pay close attention to what images and circumstances you return to often. A fantasy journal helps you understand how your mind uses fantasy—and what fantasies you often return to.

Do you use memory or fantasy to escape your reality? At what points in your reality do you use fantasy most? Is it to relieve loneliness or anxiety? Is it to get out of an uncomfortable circumstance? Observing, journaling, and analyzing your fantasies helps you become more informed for deeper awareness of your personal themes. These are wonderful to share with your therapist!

This can be a secret file in your notes on your phone, a small pocket journal, or a file on your laptop. It is fun to maintain this practice and won't take away from your usual workday—even if you are the CEO of a successful company. Fantasy journaling is for you, and it can be done as you wish. After some time exploring some of your peak fantasies, your fantasies will become richer and more communicative. Perhaps you will see your memories or fantasies in a new light. This kind of writing is delicate and personal. The most important aspect of any journaling, especially fantasy journaling, is working through the inhibitions of the mind that will hold you back—even perhaps without realizing it.

During memory and fantasy journaling, reflect upon how you are allowing yourself to take in these experiences. What comes to mind as the most adventurous? Most pleasurable? Most humiliating? What memory would you feel excited about but afraid to share with another person? Begin to write one down. Whatever moves you first to explore.

Are you allowing yourself to fully express and enjoy writing down the peak emotional moments in the imagery? Are you holding back out of fear that someone might read it? Can you let yourself access those memories or moments in fantasy clearly? Explore the emotions that have been aroused during this memory or fantasy. Did you shut yourself down when your nervous system became engaged to avoid emotion? Have you been able to identify some of your childhood wounds and traumas and how they have affected or affect your past experiences and current fantasies? Are you available to listen to your trauma and memory with compassion? Do you allow yourself to explore your passions? Have you been able to see how ingrained scripts may be holding you back from exploring your authentic desires and self? Have you begun to become aware of how to commit to necessary life-affirming changes?

What do you think about the use of some of your memories or fantasies? Do some have a more playful component? Are some more for the hopes or successes of procreation? Are some simply for relaxation—or even a desire to escape or calm down? Are some to express emotion? Which of these scenarios affect you more than others?

What else comes to mind as you write about the varying kinds of sexual experiences or uses for sex you have explored in your life thus far? Am I open to having all my thoughts and feelings, knowing that I can consciously choose my actions or nonactions?

At home now, while journaling your memories and fantasies, keep a basic question in mind: What is the theme of this memory or fantasy—and how is that personal for me?

Chapter 11
Mind and Body: Practices

In this chapter, we will discuss specific physical exercises that work with circulating life force, sensual, or Chi energy throughout your body. These Eastern healing techniques are simple and done at home in loose clothing either seated, standing, or lying flat. These energy practices can help a person who has been through trauma regain a relationship with body energy that may have become numb through rejection of the body.

These exercises also help a person who is seeking greater natural energy throughout the day for physical fitness, mental clarity, food or hunger cravings, and an overall increased positive outlook. Learning to incorporate these exercises helps you become more attuned to your body's energy and develop a mind-and-body union for total awareness and transcendence. This helps you hear intuitive guidance more clearly and feel a stronger connection to the ability to give and receive love by allowing and increasing your spontaneous flow of vital life in the present moment. I hope you enjoy them. You can try these simple, fun practices with a friend, a family member, or a partner!

Root Chakra Energy Practice

* This is a standard and simple practice in Eastern healing arts in building Chi or life force circulation in your body.

❋ They help your body maintain a much healthier state of being and a higher state of natural energy.

❋ When you do these exercises, you lock your Chi or life force energy inward and use your muscle contraction to push the energy through your body.

❋ It is done sitting on the floor in comfortable clothing.

❋ For women: At the center of your root and second chakra is your Kegel muscle. You might have heard this same exercise being called Kegel exercises. The term Kegel was derived from the name of a US doctor in the 1950s who began prescribing these exercises to people to avoid surgery for women with urinary stress incontinence.

❋ For men: At the center of your root chakra is your pubococcygeus (PC) muscle.

The best way to identify this muscle is to think about the way you try to stop the flow of urine when you need to go to the bathroom but aren't able to find a lavatory. You stop the flow by squeezing this muscle. This will strengthen and tone the muscles in your genital area, which is really healthy for a woman's uterus and a man's prostate. By doing PC pumps, women can stay away from prolapsed uterus and incontinence and men can increase their erection capacity and massage their prostate gland, which helps it stay healthy. A lot of people have issues with their prostate glands, and this is a really wonderful way to keep your body healthy.

Root chakra energy pumps are really easy to do. When you start doing these exercises, you might find that your stomach, buttocks, hips, and even jaw hold tension. The base of your spine and the top of your spine are connected to these body parts, and your PC or Kegel muscles send a flow of energy up your spine. Just notice that tension— and allow it to go. After a short while of doing these PC pumps, you will be able to isolate and contract the different muscles while keeping the rest of your body relaxed. It is important to maintain your connection with deep, relaxed breathing during the process.

☼ Inhale, contract the PC, keep your body relaxed, and hold your contraction and breath for about the count of ten. Keep the body relaxed. Slowly exhale, let go of the muscles, and sit. Do a squeeze and push as you exhale, contract Kegel or PC, keep the rest of the body relaxed, and hold contraction with breath for five.

☼ Exhale on five, push out the muscles, and repeat that ten times. Fluttering, inhale slowly and deeply into the first two chakras, contract Kegel or PC muscles, keep the rest of your body relaxed, and while you hold your breath, quickly relax and contract your Kegel or PC muscles five times.

☼ Make sure to connect your breath to your muscle movement.

☼ Slowly exhale and relax.

☼ Repeat that all ten times. Build your practice like you do for any muscle.

Do these exercises every day—you can do them anywhere. Try them when you feel tired and want a little jolt of energy. Try it when you are on the treadmill and want to feel your breath and body unite for better performance. Try it when you are making love. This simple exercise will cultivate sensitivity and natural energy in your body.

Golden Light/Active Breath Practice

☼ This exercise creates an energized breath in your body that clears mind clutter and enhances oxygen flow in your body.

☼ This practice decreases food cravings, depressive tendencies, and anxiety. This increases blood flow, positive thoughts, and energy.

☼ This exercise also helps you become more attuned to a positive experience of your life force energy or Chi.

☼ When we are holding trauma, we often need to reenergize and learn how to connect specifically with this energy in our bodies. You may have gone numb there due to shock and pain.

You can learn to listen and respond to the sensitivity of the subtle energy in these areas of your beautiful body.

✲ Wear loose clothing. Lay on the floor or bed, on your back, imagine you are flat on the earth, and feel the pulse of life force from the earth moving into your body.

✲ Place your feet flat on the floor or bed, with your knees bent, and slightly apart.

✲ Place your hands at your side with your palms up. Close your eyes.

✲ Breathe into your root and second chakra. Focus your attention inward and imagine life force energy or Chi moving through your legs, from the earth, into your first and second chakras.

✲ Slowly lift your pelvis toward the sky.

✲ Now, use your hips (not your pelvic muscles) to tilt your pelvis toward sky and then back toward the earth.

✲ Practice deep breathing as you find a steady rhythm of rocking your pelvis forward and back, toward the sky and then toward the earth.

✲ Move slowly, listen to your body, and do what feels right for your own speed. If something feels off, listen to your body first and foremost.

✲ Inhale and exhale. Make simple and gentle sounds like "ah." Are you shy about making sounds? Sound is vibration, a way to express your energetic vibration, and freedom feels really great! Just do it! Find your primal growl or meow.

✲ As you rock backward, tighten your Kegel or PC. As you rock forward, let it go.

✲ Start to visualize your life force or Chi energy as a great ball of golden fire in your pelvis.

✲ Rock forward and backward with your feet flat on the earth. Breathe, contract, and loosen your muscle. Imagine that you are drawing this golden fire ball up through your chakra centers, one chakra at a time.

✺ Send this beautiful golden, healing light of energetic vibration through your crown chakra and out into the universe for total healing of all living matter. Don't let it this energy build up in your head/mind. Imagine it moving through your crown chakra and into the universal flow of love.

✺ To aid this process, you can pass your hands over your chakra centers and use your interoception practice to mentally move the energy up through your subtle energy centers. Breathing more rapidly will allow the energy to move more freely into your higher chakras.

✺ As your body energy increases, deepen the visceral flow of natural life force or Chi through your body by slowing down your breathing. Keep your body relaxed as you tune in to this rhythm of breath, pelvic tilt, and muscle squeeze. Remember to feel the vital flow of energy from the earth up into your cells.

✺ Maintain this circulation of healing, golden life force energy through your chakras and out the top of your head as long as you want to by continuing to deepen and slow your breathing—deep and slow instead of tense and fast.

✺ When you have to stop, simply rest in this energy pool for a while.

✺ Sit still and breathe in and out. Feel your total presence in your mind-and-body union. Listen to your heartbeat. Listen to your soul or intuitive thoughts.

✺ Know that you have built up a fullness of energy in your being that you can access all day.

✺ When you stand, ground yourself. Feel your feet on the ground and reconnect yourself to the earth. If you feel pressure in your crown, place your thumbs on your crown to let the energy move out of the top of your head and into the universe. If you feel a headache, release any stunted body or mental energy from your crown.

Passion Pump Practice

This exercise combines deep breathing, root chakra energy practice, and active breath practice. It creates an energy storehouse in your belly or second chakra. It is safe to store it there. If you store energy in your head or in your root, it becomes heavy. Creating too much pressure in those subtle energy fields within your chakra system will throw off the vital flow of energy in your body. This exercise will help you keep energy moving in your body throughout the day. When you want an extra supply, put your attention on your belly or second chakra and move some out and up your circuit with breath.

✾ Wear loose clothing. Sit up comfortably in a chair. Place your feet flat on floor. Keep your back straight. Relax your shoulders. Close your eyes. Keep your arms and hands loose on your lap or at your side.

✾ Inhale slowly and count to five. Fill the bottom, middle, and upper portions of your lungs.

✾ Gently hold your breath for a count of five.

✾ Exhale through your nose for a count of five.

✾ Repeat this three times.

Repeat this while adding your root chakra energy practice, Kegel, and PC contractions:

✾ As you inhale for the fifth time, tighten your Kegel or PC muscles. Hold them tightly while you hold your breath. Relax as you exhale. Repeat this three more times (for a total of eight repetitions).

✾ On the ninth inhale, squeeze your Kegel or PC muscle. Hold your breath. Touch your teeth lightly together. Gently push your jaw straight back. You will feel a slight pull in the back of your neck.

✿ Gently roll your eyes back and up and look toward the top of your head. These subtle movements help carry energy all the way up to your crown chakra.

✿ Finally, touch the tip of your tongue to the roof of your mouth. Your tongue in this position completes the energy circuit by joining the back and front energy lines in your body.

✿ Repeat three times and leave your tongue touching the roof of your mouth for the remainder of this meditation.

✿ On your thirteenth inhale, squeeze your Kegel or PC muscle. Visualize pushing a bright beam of energy up your spine from your root and second chakra. As you push your eyes back and roll your eyes up, the energy beam gets pulled up to your crown chakra.

✿ Exhale, roll your eyes down, and relax your muscles. The energy spills over and rolls down your front channels through your third eye, tongue, throat chakra, heart, solar plexus, and belly—and back into your root.

✿ Repeat this sequence ten or fifteen times. Inhale, squeeze Kegel or PC, push energy up your spine, hold your breath, pull jaw back, eyes up, energy to the top of your head, exhale, eyes down, tongue remains touching the roof of your mouth, relax your PC muscle, and energy flows down to your legs.

✿ On your last round, as your energy is flowing down your front pathway, bring it to rest in your belly chakra. Let it rest in your belly chakra.

✿ Rest in silence for as long as you wish—and observe what is happening within your body.

Energy in your body will follow your attention. By using these visualizations, your life force or Chi energy follows the circuit your mind's eye sees within you. If you want to be especially alert and receptive during the day, you can grab some energy from your heart and send it down to your second and root chakra. Give a little Kegel or PC squeeze and use energy breath to move it up to your brain. You will get extra energy that will bring you greater alertness for artistic or physical activities or conversations. With these exercises as your daily practice, you can store energy in your belly chakra and access it at any time for all sorts of wonderful things during the day! It creates a union in your mind and body that facilitates total healing, rejuvenation, and transcendence.

Welcome to your new way of life!

Reverie: Relax on Your Back

This is a beautiful time when your unconscious mind is incredibly open, and there is an opportunity for integration between your conscious and unconscious self. Place one hand on your heart and one on your root or second chakra. Feel the natural pulse of life in your body.

Notice the images that float through your mind. Memories, fantasies, colors, thoughts, culminations of realizations, intuitive wisdoms, sense of focus, and awareness arise. Let your mind free-associate. If there are any thoughts or fantasies you want to write down later, do so.

Aftercare

Be sure to drink lots of water throughout the day. Find moments to build pockets of mindful breath, stillness, and pleasure throughout your days and nights so that attuning to this subtle energy in your mind-and-body union isn't such a far reach from your new regular state of being. Awareness is intense! Be easy with yourself and remember to laugh and play a lot! The more open you are in your subtle energy bodies, the more joy and love you can radiate! Enjoy laughter, nature, play, and positive thoughts!

Closing Thought and Prayers

Your journey has just begun. We are at the end of our book. We have discovered the foundations of breath practice, somatic awareness, mindful pleasure focus, mindful emotional attunement, heart opening, mindful removing blocks practice, chakra balancing, emotional expression, fantasy expression practices, and mind-and-body energy practices.

Spiritual Perspective

Be mindful that this book is focused directly on self. As we develop a deeper relationship with the mind and body, our relationships with others can deepen. When we feel thrown off by relationships with others, we know we need to return to our relationship to self, reintegrate, and recalibrate. This is our total responsibility, and it is the path to truly healthy and truly loving relationships.

We become mindful throughout the day of returning to the breath and body scan. Throughout this healing process, we are working toward a purification of the subtle body energy by taking care of and honoring our bodies and becoming aware of mental patterns. We begin to identify patterns of intentions and actions that work against our natural vital flow and lead us toward feeling disconnected from our bodies A mind running off into the future or the past is never healthy. We return to the present through the experience of our breath in our bodies.

Speaking from your truth—from your core integrity—is a beautiful practice. Getting in touch with your truth requires slowing down and tuning in. Following, believing in, and asserting your truth in a loving and receptive way toward others and yourself helps you survive and become fulfilled. We want to flourish in love, play, work, and service! Energy never dies; it only transforms. You create purified, love-filled energy as you heal and balance, and it vibrates out into the rest of the world. Healing yourself is doing service to the evolution of our species!

Healing and integrating your mind and body is a lifestyle! I simply ask you to, mindfully, as often as you can throughout each day, pause a moment, place one hand on your heart and one on your third or second chakra, feel your pulse in your body, and feel grateful for this life.

The more you develop your mind-and-body union, the more available you will be to your unconscious mind and the interconnection between your soul and your conscious mind. This is a beautiful place to live. It is open, vibrating, and serene. Focus on manifestation and being all at once. You can be more available and incredibly loving. There is integration between your mind and body and the conscious and unconscious.

Throughout each day, notice the images that float through your mind. Notice any memories, fantasies, colors, thoughts, culminations of realizations, intuitive wisdoms, sense of focus, and awareness that arise. Let your mind free-associate. If you have any thoughts or fantasies you want to write, do so. Be sure to drink lots of water and get proper exercise and nutrition throughout each day. Continue to find moments to build pockets of mindful breath, stillness, and pleasure. Attuning to this libidinal current is your new, natural, chosen state of being. You are healing any anxiety or trauma—your union of mind and body—for total awareness.

Closing Prayer

I would like to close with a simple prayer of appreciation. I hope you will join me. Remain with one hand placed one hand on your heart and one on the second chakra. Feel the source. Feel the life force. Feel your natural sensuality flowing through the vibrational force of your being. Imagine my voice with you.

I'd like to say a prayer of appreciation or gratitude
to the universe for this beautiful life force pulsing
through our bodies, which allows us to continue
living every moment of every day. This mysterious
force of nature makes our magnificent hearts beat.
I don't know where it came from. I don't know why.
I don't even know for how long. This mysterious
heartbeat allows us to connect with other living
beings, with ourselves, and with the spontaneous
movement of life and synchronicities. At any time,
during the day or night, we can slow down, put our
hands on our hearts or anywhere on our bodies, take
a breath, feel, and say thank you for all that we are,
all that we have, and all that we don't know. Show
gratitude for the mysteries of it all—the unknowns
of this magnificent and vast universe. Go out into
the world and spread the love. I am right there with
you! Warmth and lightness to your heart and being.

References

Anand, Margot. 1990. *The Art of Sexual Ecstasy: The Path of Sacred Sexuality for Western Lovers.*

Bataille, Geroges. 1957. *Eroticism,* translated by Mary Dalwood. London and New York: Marion Boyars, 1962 [1957].

Beres, D. 1962. *Language and the Discovery of Reality: A Developmental Psychology of Cognition by Joseph Church.* New York: Random House, Inc., 1961.

Beres D. 1962. *The Unconscious Fantasy.* Psychoanal. Q. 31, 309–328.

Bollas, C. 2004) *Cracking up: The Work of Unconscious Experience.* Taylor and Francis Ltd., London.

Caffyn, Jesse, Moore, Cassie, and Yahya Medhi. 2017. *Healers on the Edge: Somatic Sex Education.*

Cannon, W. B. 1927) "The James-Lange Theory of Emotion: A Critical Examination and an Alternative Theory." *American Journal of Psychology,* 39, 10–124.

Chun Siong Soon, Marcel Brass, Hans-Jochen Heinze, and John-Dylan Haynes, "Unconscious Determinants of Free Decisions in the Human Brain." *Nature Neuroscience,* April 13, 2008.

Dach, L Jeffrey. 2018. *Heart Book: How to Keep Your Heart Healthy: MD.* Medical Muse Press. Davie, Florida.

Damasio AR, Grabowski TJ, Bechara A, Damasio H, Ponto LL, Parvizi J, Hichwa RD. 2000. "Subcortical and cortical brain activity during the feeling of self-generated emotions." *Nature Neuroscience*.

Damasio A, Geschwind N. 1984. "The neural basis of language." *Annual Review of Neuroscience*. 7: 127–147.

Damasio, A; Carvalho, GB. 2013. "The nature of feelings: Evolutionary and neurobiological origins." Nature Reviews. *Neuroscience*. 14 (2): 143–52.

Dillman, Suzanne M. "GoodTherapy.org/LearningtoAcceptLove AfterExperiencingTrauma."

Einstein, Albert. 1916. *Relativity: The Special and General Theory* (Translation 1920. New York: H. Holt and Company.

Feinstein J, Adolphs R, Damasio A, Tranel D. 2011. *Current Biology*.

Freud, Sigmund. 1910. *Infantile Sexuality*. Three Contributions to the Sexual Theory.

Freud, Sigmund. 1911. *Formulations on the Two Principles of Mental Functioning*, translated by James Strachey, edited by Angela Richards, *On Metapsychology: The Theory of Psychoanalysis*. London: Penguin Books, 1991, 29–44.

Freud, Sigmund. 2003. *Beyond the Pleasure Principle and Other Writings*. Freud in Love, IV) Translated by John Reddick with an introduction by Mark Edmundson. Penguin Classics. London, England.

Fournier, G. 2018. "James-Lange Theory." *Psych Central*. Retrieved on September 16, 2018, from https://psychcentral.com/encyclopedia/james-lange-theory/.

Fox G.R.; Kaplan J.; Damasio H.; Damasio A. 2015. "Neural correlates of gratitude." *Frontiers in Psychology*. 6 (1491).

Grayson, Henry. 2012) *Use Your Body to Heal Your Mind: Revolutionary Methods to Release all Barriers to Health, Healing, and Happiness.* Balboa Press, Bloomington, Indiana.

Hass, Michaela. 2013. *Dakini Power.* Shambhala, Boston, Massachusetts.

Inderbitzin, L. B. and Levy, S. T. 1990. "Unconscious fantasy: A reconsideration of the concept." *Journal of the American Psychoanalytic Association,* 38 (1), 113–130.

Iyengar, BKS. 1960. *Light on Yoga: The Bible of Modern Yoga.* Pantheon Books, NY.

Kappers, CU Ariens. 1929) "The evolution of the nervous system in invertebrates, vertebrates and man" De Erven F. Bohn, Haarlem.

Kumin, I. 1996. *Guilford psychoanalysis series. Pre-object relatedness: Early attachment and the psychoanalytic situation.* New York, NY, US: Guilford Press.

Mancia, Mauro. 2006. "Implicit memory and early unrepressed unconscious: Their role in the therapeutic process." *Int J Psychoanal.* 2006 Feb; 87(Pt. 1): 83–103.

Mitrani, Judith. 1995. "Toward an Understanding of Unmentalized Experience." *The Psychoanalytic Quarterly.* 64. 68–112.

Morin, Jack. 1995. *The Erotic Mind: Unlocking the Inner Sources of Sexual Passion and Fulfillment.* HarperCollins Publishers.

Neuroscience and Biobehavioral Reviews, 36. 2012) 747–756 journal homepage: www.elsevier.com/locate/neubiorev.

Osho. 2008. *Being in Love: How to Love with Awareness and Relate Without Fear.* New York, New York: Harmony Books.

Osho. 1990. *The Dhammapada: The Way of the Buddha,* Vol. 10, New York, New York: Rebel Publ. House.

Pollack, Robert. 1999. *The Missing Moment: How the Unconscious Shapes Modern Science.* Houghton Mifflin.

Reiff, Philip. 2003. *The Mind of the Moralist, Freud, Beyond the Pleasure Principle and Other Writings. (Freud in Love,* IV) Translated by John Reddick with an introduction by Mark Edmundson. Penguin Classics. London, England.

Reiff, Philip. 1979. *The Mind of the Moralist,* Third Edition, University of Chicago Press.

Rittiner, Remo. 2010. *Big Book of Yoga Therapy: Yoga Practice for Health and Clarity.* Bookshaker.

ScienceDaily.com "Adults Demonstrate Modified Immune Response," *Science News,* September 9, 2010. Cedars-Sinai Medical Center.

Shearer, Alistair, Russell, Peter. 1990. *The Upanishads.* Mandala Books.

Silvan S. Schweber. *Journal of the History of Biology* Vol. 13, No. 2 (Autumn 1980). 195–289.

Simmer-Brown, Judith. 2001. *Dakini's Warm Breath.* Shambhala, Boston, Massachusetts.

Spillius, E. 2007. *Freud and Klein on the Concept of Phantasy,* P. Roth and R. Rusbridger (eds.) Encounters with Melanie Klein. Routledge.

Winnicott, DW. 1960. "Ego Distortion in Terms of True and False Self," *The Maturational Process and the Facilitating Environment: Studies in the Theory of Emotional Development.* New York: International UP Inc., 1960, 140–152.

Mind and Its Relation to the Psyche-Soma: The Collected Works of D. W. Winnicott: Volume 3, 1946–1951 (245) Edited by Lesley Caldwell and Helen Taylor Robinson Publisher: Oxford University Press.

"The Use of an Object." 1969. *International Journal of Psycho-Analysis*, 50:711–716.

"Primitive emotional development." 1945. *International Journal of Psycho-Analysis*, 2.Q, 137–143.

The Maturational Processes and the Facilitating Environment: Studies in the Theory of Emotional Development. 1965. London: Hogarth Press.

Transitional Objects and Transitional Phenomena in Playing and Reality (1–30). Harmondsworth: Penguin Books. 1971.

Human Nature. 1988. New York: Schocken Books.

Ogden, T. 1989. *The Primitive Edge of Experience*. Northvale, NJ: Jason Aronson,

Person, Ethel Spector, et al., editors. 1995). On Freud's "Creative Writers and Day-Dreaming." Yale University Press.

Unknown. Le Ligue de la Sainte-Messe (ed. Father Esther Bouquerel). 1912. "Prayer of Saint Francis, Belle priere a faire pendant la Messe, La Clochette."

CPSIA information can be obtained
at www.ICGtesting.com
Printed in the USA
FSHW020002251119
64388FS

9 781480 879072